BRUNCH

THE SUNDAY WAY

This book is dedicated to the life of Leonor Riel-Williamson
who was a founding member of Sunday! Leonor look what we did…
we hope we have made you proud.

BRUNCH

THE SUNDAY WAY

Alan Turner + Terence Williamson

Photography by Patricia Niven

FRANCES LINCOLN

Contents

//

Introduction

Although *Sunday* originally opened as a restaurant focusing on dinner, brunch has always been at the heart of what we do and love. From the moment we opened our doors in July 2013, we have been fortunate enough to have a constant stream of brunch-loving customers, and this has only increased over time.

We are both career chefs, and between us have a combined experience of over 40 years working in busy kitchens (with the grey hairs to prove it). We met in one of those kitchens, and after connecting over a love of food – and an itch to be our own bosses – we decided to open *Sunday*. It was a giant leap into the unknown, but one we have never regretted, and the warm reception we received from our wonderful neighbours in Islington played a huge part in that. Our ethos was – and remains – serving generous portions of good food, made with seasonal, locally sourced produce.

We were part of the early wave of 'proper' brunch destinations in London, who took it seriously as a legitimate meal, as opposed to something that was an accidental overhang from breakfast. We observed that brunch was being done elsewhere, but not as well as we would like, so we made it part of our mission to change that. We always wanted *Sunday* to be the kind of establishment where we would want to take our own family and friends, and that remains our guiding principle.

Looking back, our first brunch service was the perfect example of how popular it would become: overwhelmed by demand we weren't expecting, we found ourselves having to serve smaller and smaller portions in order to be able to continue serving customers to the end of the day. Both delighted and dismayed by how spectacularly we had underestimated the footfall of hungry brunchers, we ditched our plans to open for a dinner service that evening and decided to prep for the following day's brunch service instead. We chuckle about it now, but it was an experience we haven't repeated since.

Opening day adventures aside, thankfully we were extremely well received by our local neighbourhood, and word soon spread to the wider public. It quickly became clear that brunch was the way forward; the demand for it was never-ending, and we could see how its place in food culture was changing at breakneck speed to become 'the' meal of the day. So we decided

to stop serving dinner and switch to focusing solely on brunch. It was the right decision: we got our lives back (much to our relief) and could also dedicate our efforts to satisfying the crowd of brunch-lovers.

At *Sunday*, we focus on doing the classics well, with a modern twist and a respect for seasonal produce. As an independent business, we are proud to support other local independents and source from them whenever we can. As a result, we have access to exceptional produce which makes great food. Our menu is constantly changing to reflect seasonal ingredients and whatever inspires us. The result is a range of creative, flavoursome, and varied dishes, incorporating international influences, and providing plenty of choice for sweet and savoury brunchers alike.

This book is a collection of our favourite and best brunch dishes of all time. It is a reflection of our menu archives over the last six years and includes both Sunday classics, which always feature on our menu – such as our much-photographed pancakes and French toast – as well as some of our popular weekly specials. We have also shared our recipes for delicious sauces and jams, because it really does make a difference when you make these from scratch.

Why write a book solely about brunch? Apart from the fact that it is – literally – our bread and butter, it also celebrates what is arguably the most joyous meal of the day. We felt brunch came out of nowhere, and as such has been able to make up its own rules; it can be enjoyed any time of day; it can be entirely sweet or savoury, or both in equal measure (a savoury dish followed by a half/full stack of pancakes is a popular choice at Sunday); it can be easy or complex; it can be a social 'event', bringing people together or a casual, laid-back affair. More than anything, to us brunch is fun, which is what good food should be.

Our goal here is to encourage food lovers to create a brunch experience at home and prove that even the more complicated dishes are within reach. It has been incredible for us to adapt our dishes into something accessible and easy to make in your own kitchens, whilst faithfully replicating what we produce in the restaurant. As well as sharing recipes for getting the core brunch basics right (poached eggs, hollandaise, the simple yet awesome avocado on toast), we have included tips we use in the restaurant to make our – and your – lives easier. Often, elements of a dish can be prepared in advance, and we flag up where this can be done. These tips can make a big difference to the time and effort required when you want to sit down and eat quickly. In terms of ingredients, we would encourage you to explore what local produce your neighbourhood offers and buy the best that you can.

The highest compliment would be to know that this book has become a solid guide for brunching outside the box; one that is well-used, engaged with, scribbled with notes, and encourages confidence to adapt the recipes and make them your own. At *Sunday*, brunch is all about creative, super tasty food made with passion and enjoyed in a warm, lively atmosphere. Nothing would make us happier than to know that this book has enabled you to do the same in your own home.

Eggs the Sunday Way

Classic Poached Eggs

//

Poached eggs can be quite daunting, and most people we speak with are genuinely nervous about attempting them. But really, it's not so scary. It's simply about the freshness and quality of the eggs. Make sure you use the freshest eggs you can, as old eggs won't hold together while poaching, and preferably use organic eggs.

The vinegar is also essential to get a good poached egg – don't attempt to make them without it as your poached eggs will be flat and sad, and you won't get that awesome tear drop shape. And don't be fooled into fiercely boiling the water – a gentle simmer is key so the bubbling doesn't break up the eggs.

You can cook your eggs in advance, too. This can be done the night before if you have a brunch planned for the next day. It really does take the stress away from cooking breakfast for groups. Just store the poached eggs in a bowl of water in the fridge.

SERVES / 4
TIME TAKEN / 10 minutes

4 tbsp white wine vinegar
4 very fresh large eggs

Bring a large, deep pan of water to a gentle simmer and add the white wine vinegar. Don't have the water boiling too fiercely or it will break up the eggs. Crack the eggs into 4 separate small bowls, each deep enough to hold 1 egg.

Stir the water gently to create a whirlpool. Carefully add the eggs from the small bowls one at a time, spacing them out around the pan. After a few seconds the white should start to set around the yolk of the egg and create a tear drop shape. Cook the eggs for 3½ minutes, then remove from the pan with a slotted spoon. Drain on kitchen paper, them trim off any untidy excess white before serving.

POACHING EGGS FOR REHEATING LATER
If you are poaching the eggs for a dish to be made later, have a deep plastic container with ice water at the ready.

Follow the instructions above, but cook the eggs for just 2½ minutes. Remove them from the pan and place into the container of ice water to shock cool them – this will keep the yolks nice and runny for when you are ready to use them.

To reheat the pre-poached eggs, place them in a pan of simmering water for 2 minutes, then remove with slotted spoon, drain on kitchen paper and serve.

Crispy Poached Eggs

//

SERVES / 2

TIME TAKEN / 20 minutes

2 large eggs, plus 1 beaten egg
4 tbsp plain flour
100g (3½oz) panko breadcrumbs
sunflower oil, for deep frying
sea salt and black pepper

Start by getting a bowl of iced water ready. Pre-poach the eggs for 2½ minutes, according to the method on page 14, then plunge them straight into the iced water to cool down. Once they are cold, remove the eggs from the water and place on a clean tea towel. Gently dry them.

Place the flour in a shallow bowl and season with salt and pepper. Put the beaten egg into a second shallow bowl, and put the panko breadcrumbs into a third bowl. Handling the eggs gently, coat them first in flour, then in beaten egg, and then in panko breadcrumbs, shaking off any excess after each stage.

Pour sunflower oil into a small heavy-based pan to a depth of 5cm (2in). Heat it to 180°C / 350°F over a medium heat. Test the oil's temperature by gently dropping in a small piece of bread; it should sizzle and start to brown but not blacken. If the oil is too hot, remove from the heat and allow to cool until you pass the golden bread test.

Carefully lower the crumbed eggs into the oil using a slotted spoon and cook for 1–2 minutes until golden brown, turning if necessary to ensure they are evenly cooked. Remove from the oil with the slotted spoon and drain on kitchen paper.

Son-in-Law Eggs

//

SERVES / 2
TIME TAKEN / 30 minutes

2 eggs
30g (1¼oz) plain flour
500ml (17fl oz) rapeseed oil
sea salt and black pepper

Get a small pan of water boiling and add the eggs. Cook for 6 minutes, then refresh them under running cold water,

While the eggs are still a little warm, peel them – the shell will come off easier than when they are cold. As the eggs will still be soft in the middle, you'll need to take care as they need to remain whole and unbroken. Once peeled, keep in cold water until needed.

Put the flour into a small bowl and season with salt and pepper.

Gently remove an egg from the water and carefully shake off excess water. Carefully roll it in the flour to coat the whole egg. Place on a plate lined with kitchen paper, and repeat the process to coat the other egg.

Put the oil in a small heavy-based pan – it needs to be deep enough to cover the eggs, so that they float and don't sit on the bottom, or they may burn. Heat the oil over medium heat to 170°C / 325°F. If you don't have a thermometer, you can test it's hot enough by dropping a small piece of white bread into the oil; it should sizzle and turn golden brown. If it colours too quickly, lower the heat and allow to cool slightly.

Add the floured eggs to the oil and cook for 3–4 minutes, turning often to get an even golden colour around the whole egg. Once golden, remove from the pan using a slotted spoon and place onto kitchen paper to drain of excess oil.

The son-in-law eggs are ready to serve. When you cut them open you should find the most delicious runny egg yolks. Enjoy.

Scrambled Eggs
on Toasted Sourdough

//

SERVES / 2

TIME TAKEN / 20 minutes

5 large eggs
3 tbsp double cream
a pinch of sea salt
20g (¾oz) unsalted butter, plus extra for spreading
2 thick slices sourdough bread, to serve

FOR THE TOMATOES

2 plum vine tomatoes
1 sprig of thyme
1 garlic clove
1 tbsp olive oil, plus extra for drizzling
sea salt and black pepper

Preheat the oven to 170°C fan/190°C/ 375°F/gas 5 and line a small baking tray with parchment.

Cut the tomatoes in half lengthways and place on the prepared baking tray. Season with salt and pepper, add the thyme and garlic, and drizzle with the 1 tablespoon of olive oil. Roast for 15 minutes until lightly coloured and just cooked.

Crack the eggs into a mixing bowl and whisk for a few minutes until the eggs are well beaten. Add the cream and salt and mix again until fully incorporated.

Put the butter into a non-stick frying pan and gently melt over a low heat. Add the beaten eggs and continue to stir using a wooden spoon for 6–8 minutes, cooking until the eggs become light and fluffy, but are still quite moist. It's important to not overcook the eggs or they will become dry.

While the eggs are scrambling, toast the bread and butter generously.

To assemble, place a slice of toast on each plate and divide the scrambled eggs between the slices. Place the roasted tomatoes on the side, drizzle with olive oil and serve.

Feta, Kale and Quinoa Omelette

///

50g (1¾oz) kale, stems removed and discarded
30g (1¼oz) quinoa
6 large eggs
50g (1¾oz) feta cheese, roughly crumbled
2 tbsp rapeseed oil
sea salt and black pepper

TO SERVE
1 avocado
60g (2oz) mixed salad leaves (we like rocket, baby spinach, watercress and ruby chard)
a drizzle of extra virgin olive oil
2 slices good-quality sourdough bread
butter, for spreading
Beetroot and Dill Purée (see page 144)
25g (1oz) shaved Parmesan cheese

Preheat the oven to 160°C fan/180°C/350°F/gas 4.

Bring a pan of water to a rolling boil and add a good pinch of salt. Add the kale leaves and blanch for 1 minute. Remove with a slotted spoon, retaining the cooking water, and plunge into a bowl of iced cold water (this will stop it from over cooking and keeps the colour vibrant). Drain, roughly chop and set aside.

To cook the quinoa, rinse well, then add it to the pan of water used for the kale and bring back to a rolling boil. Reduce the heat, and simmer for 15 minutes or until tender. Drain and set aside.

For each omelette, crack 3 eggs into a bowl and whisk. Add half of the feta, blanched kale and cooked quinoa to each bowl and season to taste.

Heat 1 tablespoon of rapeseed oil in a 15 cm (6 in) non-stick omelette pan with a wooden handle over a medium heat. When the oil is hot, add a bowl of the egg mixture to the pan, making sure the ingredients are evenly spread across the base. Transfer the pan to the preheated oven and cook for 6–8 minutes until the eggs are just set. Remove the omelette from the pan and cover with foil. Add another tablespoon of oil to the pan and repeat using the other bowl of egg mixture. (If you have 2 pans, you could cook them simultaneously.)

While the omelettes are cooking, thinly slice the avocado and season with salt and pepper.

Dress the salad leaves with a drizzle of olive oil. Toast the sourdough bread, then spread with butter.

Once both omelettes are cooked, slide each onto a serving plate. Place half the avocado on one half of the omelettes, a spoonful of the beetroot and dill purée and the salad leaves on the other half. Sprinkle the leaves with shaved Parmesan and serve with the toast.

Salt Cod Potato Benedict
with Poached Eggs and Hollandaise

///

SERVES / 2

TIME TAKEN / 3 hours, plus overnight preparation for the cod

300g (10½ oz) skinless cod fillet
200g (7oz) table salt
350g (12oz) Maris Piper potatoes, peeled and chopped into even-sized pieces
4 spring onions, finely sliced
30g (1¼ oz) flat leaf parsley, chopped
grated zest of ½ lemon
plain flour, for dusting
vegetable oil, for frying
4 Poached Eggs (see page 14)
a knob of butter
150g (5½ oz) baby spinach
1 recipe quantity Hollandaise Sauce (see page 157)
sea salt and black pepper

TO GARNISH
1 handful of baby watercress
olive oil, to drizzle

Start by preparing the salt cod the night before. Place the cod in a shallow dish that snugly accommodates it (you can cut the fillet into pieces). Pour over enough salt to cover the fish completely. Cover and refrigerate overnight.

The next day, rinse all the salt off the fish. Discard the salt and liquid that will have collected in the dish and rinse it out. Place the fish back in the dish, cover with fresh cold water and refrigerate for an hour. Drain off and repeat. Drain the fish again and pat dry.

Bring a small pan of water to the boil, then turn the heat down until the water is at a low simmer and add the cod. Poach gently for 5–6 minutes, or until just cooked. Transfer to a plate and allow to cool slightly then, using a fork, gently break the cod into small flakes. Set aside until needed.

For the fishcakes, put the potatoes in a pan, cover with water and add a pinch of salt. Bring the water to the boil, then cook for 15–20 minutes, or until tender but not breaking up. Drain the potatoes and leave to steam dry in a colander for a couple of minutes before returning to the pan. Over the lowest heat possible, allow the potatoes to dry out for another 1–2 minutes then mash the potatoes until you have a lumpy, fluffy mash. Empty the mash into a large bowl and allow to cool before adding the salt cod chunks, spring onions, parsley, lemon zest and black pepper to taste.

Dust your hands and a chopping board with flour and carefully shape the potato mixture into two round patties around 3cm (1¼in) thick. Chill the fishcakes for about 30 minutes to firm up.

Heat a little oil in a heavy-based frying pan over a medium heat. Fry the fishcakes for around 5 minutes on each side, or until golden and crispy. Remove from the pan and keep warm in the oven on a low heat.

Poach the eggs as per the recipe on page 14.

Wipe down the frying pan, then add the knob of butter and melt over a medium-high heat. Add the spinach and cook for a couple of minutes until wilted, then season with salt and pepper. Remove the pan from the heat and drain the spinach in a strainer, gently squeezing out any excess water.

Place a fishcake on each of two plates. Top with half of the spinach and 2 poached eggs, then cover with a generous amount of hollandaise sauce. Garnish with some baby watercress and a drizzle of olive oil and serve.

White Corn Arepas with Fried Eggs

//

Remember to soak the beans the night before you want to make this dish. The salsa can be prepared in advance and left in the fridge until you are ready to use it. How to tell if plantain are ripe? They will look dark and bruised – seems counterintuitive if you're comparing them to bananas, but these are the ones you're looking for.

vegetable oil, for frying
1 ripe plantain, sliced lengthways into six pieces
1 tbsp rapeseed oil
2 chorizo cooking sausages, each sliced into 4 pieces
4 eggs

FOR THE AREPAS

250ml (9fl oz) warm water
  (hotter than hand hot but not boiling)
½ tsp sea salt
130g (4½oz) masarepa or pre-cooked maize flour
  (see note overleaf)
½ tsp baking powder

FOR THE TOMATO, AVOCADO AND
BLACK BEAN SALSA

100g (3½oz) dried black turtle beans, soaked in a
  bowl of cold water in the fridge overnight or 1 x
  400g (14oz) tin black beans, drained and rinsed
8 cherry tomatoes, halved
1 avocado, peeled, stoned and finely diced
2 spring onions, finely sliced
½ small bunch fresh coriander, chopped
½ small red onion, finely diced
1 red chilli, deseeded and finely chopped
3½ tbsp olive oil
zest and juice of 1 lime
sea salt and black pepper

If you're using dried beans, drain the soaked beans and rinse them. Put them in a pan with enough fresh water to cover the beans by about 2.5cm (1in). Bring to a boil, then turn down the heat. Simmer for about 45 minutes until soft – you should be able to squash a bean between your fingers. Turn off the heat and leave to cool in the water.

Once the beans are cool, drain and give them a quick rinse. Put them in a bowl with the remaining salsa ingredients and mix together until combined. Store in the fridge until needed.

Preheat the oven to 100°C fan/120°C/250°F/gas 1 and line a baking tray with parchment.

Mix the water and salt together in a large bowl until the salt has dissolved. Combine the masarepa and the baking powder, then start adding this to the water a little at a time, mixing together as you go with your free hand (you will eventually need both hands once the dough really starts coming together). You are looking for a smooth dough that doesn't easily stick to your hands, is pliable and moist, and can be easily rolled into a ball. You may end up using all of the masarepa, but you may get the desired consistency before you've added the full quantity. Cover the bowl with a tea towel and leave it to rest. The dough will continue to absorb water while it rests, so check it again after 10 minutes to see if it is still pliable and soft. If it feels a bit dry and hard to the touch, add a couple more tablespoons of warm water, knead again gently, re-cover, and leave to rest at room temperature until needed.

When you're ready to make the arepas, grab a large handful of the dough and, using your hands, roll it into a ball. Press the ball gently between your palms to form a disc roughly 1cm thick. If it cracks a lot at the sides, the dough may still be too dry and need more water. If so, add 1–2 tablespoons more warm water and knead the dough again to incorporate, as per the previous step. If it just cracks a little around the edges, that's fine – just close the cracks by gently pressing them together with your fingers. Once you have got a smooth round disc, repeat with the remaining dough until you have 2 large arepas.

Heat a large cast iron or non-stick pan over a medium–high heat. Once hot, add a little vegetable oil and swirl to coat the bottom of the pan. Add the arepas to the pan, leaving a little room in between each one so they don't touch. Cook for 5–6 minutes until they are golden-brown and a crust has formed (a few blackened spots are OK). Flip over and cook for a further 5–6 minutes or until the other side is also browned. Place the arepas on the lined baking tray and keep warm in the low oven while you prepare the remaining elements.

Wipe down the pan and heat 1–2 tablespoons oil on a medium-high heat. Once the oil is hot, add the slices of plantain and cook for a couple of minutes on each side until golden brown and crispy. Watch them closely to prevent them from burning, as they catch easily. Transfer to the oven to keep warm with the arepas.

Wipe down the pan again, add the rapeseed oil and place back over a medium-high heat. Add the chorizo slices to the pan and cook for 2–3 minutes on each side until they have deepened in colour. Remove from the pan and keep warm in the oven with the arepas and plantain.

Wipe down the pan again and add a small amount of oil. Crack the eggs into the pan and fry to your liking.

Now assemble the arepa. Place 2 eggs on each plate and top with some of the salsa. Place 3 slices of plantain and 4 slices of chorizo on each plate, and finish off with the warm arepa and serve. The arepa can be split along the edge and stuffed with everything on your plate to make a delicious breakfast sandwich.

NOTE / *You can find arepa flour in international supermarkets or the world food aisle of large supermarkets. Yellow or white is fine. We use the PAN brand.*

Huevos Rancheros with Spicy Black Beans and Roast Corn Salsa

//

SERVES / 2

TIME TAKEN / 1 hour

6 tbsp Spicy Black Beans (see opposite)
1 tbsp olive oil
½ small Spanish onion, finely diced
2 garlic cloves, finely chopped
1 sprig of thyme
3 cherry tomatoes, halved
200g (7oz) good-quality tinned chopped tomatoes

4 tbsp rapeseed oil
6 fresh Mexican corn tortillas
2 eggs
4 tbsp Roast Corn Salsa (see page 145)
4 sprigs fresh coriander
1 avocado, sliced
sea salt and black pepper

Preheat the oven to 160°C fan/180°C/350°F/gas 4. Heat the black beans in a small pan over a low heat.

Heat a small pan over a medium heat and add the olive oil and onion. Cook for 1 minute, then add the garlic and thyme. Cook for a further 2–3 minutes until the onion is lightly coloured and softened.

Add the cherry and chopped tomatoes, season with salt and pepper, stir well and lower the heat to medium–low. Cook for 15–20 minutes, stirring occasionally, until you have a rich tomato sauce. Remove the thyme and discard.

Put 2 tablespoons of the rapeseed oil into a small bowl and, using a pastry brush, lightly brush both sides of the corn tortillas. Cut 2 of the tortillas into wedges then place all of the them on a large non-stick baking tray (use two trays if you need to) and bake for 8–12 minutes until slightly golden and crisp.

Remove the whole tortillas from the tray onto a cooling rack. The centre of the tortillas may still be a bit soft, but they will crisp up once they cool down. Leave the tortilla wedges to cool on the baking tray.

For the eggs, heat a frying pan over a medium heat and add the remaining 2 tablespoons rapeseed oil. Once hot enough to fry, crack 2 eggs into the pan and fry to your liking.

Serve 2 whole tortillas per person and top with the black beans and tomato sauce. Place a fried egg on top of each plate and add 2 tablespoons of corn salsa and a couple of sprigs of coriander. Serve with sliced avocado and a bowl of the tortilla chips to dip in your fried egg.

Spicy Black Beans

//

SERVES / 4–6

TIME TAKEN / 2¼ hours, plus overnight soaking

250g (9oz) dried black beans, soaked in a bowl of cold water in the fridge overnight
or 2 x 400g (14oz) tin black beans, drained and rinsed
3 tbsp olive oil
1 small Spanish onion, finely diced
3 garlic cloves, finely chopped
2 tsp ground cumin
½ small chipotle chilli, finely chopped
1 x 400g (14oz) tin good-quality chopped tomatoes
1 tsp sea salt
½ tsp black pepper
1 small bunch coriander, roughly chopped

First drain the soaked black beans then rinse them under cold water for 1 minute. Put them in a pan and add 1 litre (35fl oz) of water. Set the pan over a medium heat and cook for 45 minutes.

While the beans are cooking, heat a small non-stick frying pan over a medium heat, add the oil, onion and garlic, and sauté for 2–3 minutes until softened. Add the cumin and chilli and sauté for a further 2 minutes.

After 45 minutes, add the onion mix to the beans, along with the tomatoes. Season with the salt and pepper and reduce to a low heat so that the beans are simmering.

Cook for a further 1 hour 15 minutes, stirring occasionally, until the beans are soft.

Once the beans are cooked, stir in the chopped coriander and serve.

Merguez Sausage with Tahini Flatbreads and Poached Eggs

//

SERVES / 2

TIME TAKEN / 50 minutes

olive oil, for brushing
6 good-quality merguez sausages
4 Poached Eggs (see page 14)
4 Tahini and Honey Flatbreads (see page 123)
4 tbsp Labneh (see page 142)
1 small avocado, halved, stoned and peeled

FOR THE CHILLI SAUCE
6 red chillies, deseeded
1 garlic clove
1½ tbsp apple cider vinegar
100ml olive oil
¼ tsp ground cumin
½ bunch of fresh coriander, plus extra to garnish
1 vine tomato, quartered
1 tsp soft light brown sugar
½ tsp sea salt
black pepper

Start by making the chilli sauce. Toast the chillies in a small non-stick frying pan over a high heat for a few minutes until they start to blister. Add the garlic and 150ml (5fl oz) water, reduce the heat and simmer for 3–5 minutes until the water has halved in volume. Remove from the heat and allow to cool for 10 minutes.

Place the chilli water into a food processor, add the cider vinegar, olive oil, cumin, coriander and tomato. Add the sugar and season with salt and pepper. Blend until you have a sauce with a pulpy texture – it doesn't need to be completely smooth. Put the chilli sauce into a small serving bowl and set aside until needed.

Preheat the grill to high. Have a small pot of simmering water ready to cook the eggs.

Brush a small non-stick oven tray with olive oil, place the sausages on the tray with space in between each one and grill for 10–15 minutes, turning every few minutes until they are golden.

Cook the eggs as per the recipe on page 14.

Warm the flatbreads in the oven for a couple of minutes.

To assemble, spread 2 tablespoons of labneh across the centre of each plate, thinly slice the avocado and lay it on top of the labneh. Criss cross the merguez sausages across each plate, add 2 poached eggs and drizzle with the chilli sauce. Serve with the flat breads and garnish with a few sprigs of coriander.

Crab Baked Eggs

//

*These baked eggs can be served with toast instead of cornbread, but if you have
the time and fancy the indulgence, the cornbread brings together the classic
combination of corn and crab, which work very well together.*

SERVES / 2

TIME TAKEN / 30 minutes

butter, for greasing
2 tbsp olive oil
1 small head fennel, finely sliced
1 garlic clove, finely chopped
20g (¾oz) baby spinach
1 tsp fresh dill, finely chopped
300ml (10fl oz) double cream
20g (¾oz) Parmesan cheese, grated
grated zest of ½ lemon
2 eggs
4 slices Cornbread (see page 113)
Chipotle and Maple Butter (see page 113)
100g (3½oz) fresh white crabmeat
sea salt and black pepper
chopped chives, to serve

Preheat the oven to 160°C fan/180°C/350°F/gas 4.
Grease two 225ml (8oz) ramekins with butter.

Heat a large non-stick frying pan over a medium
heat. Add the olive oil and fennel and sauté
for 3–4 minutes until lightly coloured. Add the
garlic and cook for a further 1–2 minutes. Add the
spinach and dill and cook until the spinach has
wilted. Add the double cream, Parmesan and
lemon zest, and bring to the boil. Cook for 1 minute
until slightly thickened, then remove from the
heat. Season with a pinch of salt and pepper.

Distribute the creamy spinach and fennel mixture
between the two prepared ramekins. Crack an egg
into each ramekin and place them on a baking
tray. Bake for around 12–15 minutes, or until the
whites have set and the yolks are soft (cook for
longer if you like firm yolks).

Just before the eggs are finished cooking, toast
the slices of cornbread and spread with the
chipotle and maple butter.

When the eggs are done to your liking, remove
from the oven and divide the crab meat between
the ramekins. Sprinkle with chopped chives
and serve with the toasted cornbread.

Aubergine, Tomato and Harissa Baked Eggs with Tahini and Honey Flatbreads

//

SERVES / 2

TIME TAKEN / 50 minutes

1 small aubergine, diced into
1cm (½ in) cubes
1 red pepper, cut in half and
deseeded
4 tbsp olive oil, plus extra for
drizzling
1 small onion, finely diced
2 garlic cloves, crushed
½ tsp ground cumin
½ tsp smoked paprika
8 ripe vine cherry tomatoes
1 x 400g (14oz) tin chopped tomatoes
zest of 1 lemon
2 tbsp Harissa (see page 140)
1 tsp sugar
1 handful of baby spinach
1 handful of fresh coriander,
chopped
4 eggs
sea salt and black pepper

TO SERVE

2 Tahini and Honey Flatbreads
(see page 123)
Greek yoghurt

Preheat the oven to 160°C fan/180°C/350°F/gas 4 and line a large baking tray with parchment.

Put the diced aubergine in a bowl with the pepper halves, drizzle with 2 tablespoons of the olive oil, and season with salt and pepper. Toss it all together until the vegetables are evenly coated, then spread them out on the prepared baking tray. Roast for 15–20 minutes, turning the aubergine halfway through cooking, until the aubergine is golden brown and the skin on the red pepper is charred and soft. Remove the vegetables from the oven and allow to cool enough to handle. Using the edge of a sharp knife, scrape the skin off the red pepper, discard and finely slice the flesh.

Heat the remaining olive oil in a pan over medium heat. Add the onion and garlic and sauté for 5 minutes, or until the onion is translucent. Add the cumin and paprika and cook for a further 1 minute. Push the onion and garlic mixture to one side of the pan, turn up the heat slightly, and add the cherry tomatoes along with a drizzle of olive oil. Cook the tomatoes until the skin starts to blister. Add the chopped tomatoes and lemon zest, reduce the heat, and simmer for 15–20 minutes until slightly thickened.

Add the harissa and sugar, along with the roasted aubergine and pepper, and bring back to a simmer. Add the spinach and coriander, reserving some for garnish, and cook for a couple of minutes until the spinach has wilted. Season to taste.

Divide the mixture into two ovenproof dishes (or, if you prefer, one large dish). Using the back of a spoon, make four indentations in the tomato mixture, two in each dish. Crack an egg into each indentation. Place the dishes in the oven and cook for 10–12 minutes until the egg whites are cooked and the yolks are soft, or to your liking. Check them from time to time as you don't want to overcook the yolks.

Warm the flatbreads in the oven for a couple of minutes. Serve the baked eggs with the reserved chopped coriander, flatbreads and a bowl of yoghurt.

English Breakfast Baked Eggs

//

Baked eggs are very popular as a Middle Eastern-style brunch. Here, we've given them a twist, inspired by the traditional fry-up, so you have an English breakfast in one dish. Use heatproof bowls for homely, individual servings.

SERVES / 2
TIME TAKEN / 45 minutes

2 good-quality pork sausages
2 tbsp rapeseed oil
4 eggs
1 tbsp butter
50g (1¾oz) mixed wild mushrooms, sliced
buttered sourdough toast, to serve

FOR THE TOMATO SAUCE
1 tbsp rapeseed oil
4 rashers streaky bacon, finely sliced
½ onion, finely chopped
2 garlic cloves, finely chopped
1 x 400g (14oz) tin chopped tomatoes
1 sprig thyme
½ tbsp caster sugar
2 handfuls of baby spinach
sea salt and black pepper

First, make the tomato sauce. Heat the oil in a large pan over a medium heat and fry the sliced bacon for 6–8 minutes until it is golden brown. Add the chopped onion and garlic to the pan and fry for another 3 minutes until the onion is soft.

Add the chopped tomatoes, thyme and caster sugar and season with salt and pepper. Turn the heat down and gently cook for 15 minutes until the sauce has thickened slightly. Set the sauce aside while you prepare the sausage meatballs.

Preheat the oven to 160°C fan/180°C/350°F/gas 4. Remove the sausage meat from the skins and roll it into 6 meatballs.

Heat 1 tablespoon of the rapeseed oil in a frying pan over a medium heat. Add the meatballs and gently fry them for about 5 minutes, turning during cooking, until they are evenly browned.

Reheat the tomato sauce until it is hot, then stir in the baby spinach so it wilts in the heat. Divide the sauce between two heatproof bowls, and add 3 meatballs to each one. Crack 2 eggs into each bowl. Place the bowls in the preheated oven and cook for about 15 minutes, or until the egg whites are firm and the yolks are soft.

While the eggs are baking, prepare the wild mushrooms. Heat the butter and the remaining 1 tablespoon oil in a frying pan over a medium heat. Add the mushrooms and fry for about 5 minutes, or until golden brown.

Remove the baked eggs from the oven and scatter half the mushrooms over each dish. Serve with buttered sourdough toast.

Toast
the
Sunday
Way

Mushrooms and Spinach
on Sourdough Toast

//

SERVES / 2

TIME TAKEN / 45 minutes

4 Portabello mushrooms
2 tbsp rapeseed oil
60g (2oz) Rosemary Butter (see page 151)
50g (1¾oz) baby spinach
2 Poached Eggs (see page 14)
2 slices of sourdough bread
30g (1¼oz) rocket
½ tsp olive oil
25g (1oz) Parmesan cheese, shaved
sea salt and black pepper

FOR THE WHITE BEAN PURÉE
1 x 400g (14oz) tin cannelini beans, drained and rinsed
juice of ½ lemon
1 garlic clove
3 tbsp olive oil

Preheat the oven to 170°C fan/190°C/375°F/gas 5.

First, make the white bean purée. Put all of the ingredients in a blender and blitz until smooth. Season with salt then place in a small pan over a low heat for 6–8 minutes until hot, stirring regularly to prevent it from catching. Set aside.

Peel the outer skin from the mushrooms, discard it, then gently wash the mushrooms lightly with cold water to remove any dirt. Pat dry with kitchen paper. Slice the mushrooms to your desired thickness and set aside.

Heat the rapeseed oil in a large non-stick frying pan over a high heat. Add the mushrooms and sauté for 6–8 minutes, tossing every couple of minutes. Carefully drain off any excess water that the mushrooms release. Add the rosemary butter to the mushrooms and continue to sauté for 2 minutes, then add the baby spinach and allow to wilt for a minute or so. Season with salt and pepper.

Prepare the poached eggs as per the recipe on page 14. While the eggs are poaching, toast the sourdough slices.

To assemble, spread 2 tablespoons of purée over each piece of toast. Spoon the mushrooms and spinach over the top of the toast slices, then place a poached egg on top. Lightly dress the rocket with the olive oil and place on top of the mushrooms. Sprinkle over the shaved Parmesan and serve.

Smoked Haddock Rarebit

//

300g (10½oz) undyed smoked haddock fillet, skinned
1 bay leaf
1 garlic clove
3 sprigs fresh thyme
100ml (3½fl oz) whole milk
25g (1oz) unsalted butter
½ small leek, thinly sliced (remove dark green top and discard)
25g (1oz) plain flour
50g (1¾oz) mature Cheddar cheese, grated
½ tsp Dijon mustard
½ tsp ground white pepper
2 thick slices sourdough bread

TO SERVE
2 Poached eggs (see page 14)
6 rashers dry-cured streaky bacon (optional), grilled until crisp
2 roasted plum tomatoes (see page 19)
30g (1¼oz) watercress

Preheat the oven 170°C fan/190°C/375°F/gas 5. Put the haddock into a pan, add the bay leaf, garlic and thyme, then cover with the milk. Bring to a simmer, then gently poach for 3 minutes until just cooked. Gently remove the fish from the pan and set aside to cool then gently break into large flakes using a fork. Strain the milk to remove the bay leaf, thyme and garlic, and reserve the milk.

Melt the butter in a non-stick pan over a low heat. Once melted, add the leek and sweat for 2–3 minutes until softened but not browned. Add the flour and stir in, and cook for 2 minutes to cook out the flour. Gradually add the reserved milk to the pan – it's important to not add the milk too quickly as you need to constantly stir the pan to prevent lumps. The béchamel should be thick, so that it won't run off the toast when you assemble the rarebit.

Once you have a smooth thick béchamel, add the Cheddar, mustard and pepper. Stir until the cheese has melted, then remove from the heat and gently fold in the flakes of haddock, being careful to not over mix as the fish will break down and you'll lose some texture.

Preheat the grill to high. To assemble the rarebit, toast the sourdough until golden brown on both sides (do not under-toast the bread as the rarebit will make it soggy if it's not crisp enough). Spread 2–3 tablespoons of the rarebit mix evenly over the toast, making sure to cover all the edges so that the corners don't burn when grilling. Scatter over the remaining cheese, dividing it evenly between the slices. Grill for 6–8 minutes, or until golden brown, then remove from the grill. Serve with a poached egg, bacon and tomatoes, and top with watercress.

Chilli Avocado on Sourdough with Lemony Rocket and Seeded Crackers

///

SERVES / 2

TIME TAKEN / 1¾ hours

2 ripe avocados, halved, stoned and peeled
1 tsp dried chilli flakes
juice of ½ lemon
2 tbsp olive oil, plus extra for drizzling
50g (1¾oz) rocket
2 slices sourdough bread
sea salt and black pepper

FOR THE SEEDED CRACKERS

30g (1¼oz) pumpkin seeds
30g (1¼oz) sunflower seeds
35g (1½oz) golden linseeds
1 tbsp poppy seeds
1 tsp sumac
1 tsp mustard seeds
35g (1½oz) white sesame seeds
40g (1½oz) quinoa
35g (1½oz) black sesame seeds
1 tsp sea salt
½ tsp black pepper
175ml (5½fl oz) warm water

To make the seeded crackers, place all the ingredients in a small bowl and add the warm water. Mix well and set aside for 45 minutes, mixing every 10 minutes.

Preheat the oven to 160°C fan/180°C/350°F/gas 4 and line a baking tray measuring approximately 30 x 25cm (12 x 10in) with parchment.

Spread the seed mix thinly and evenly across the surface of the prepared tray. Bake the crackers for 40–50 minutes until crisp, firm and golden brown on both sides. Remove from the oven and allow to cool on the tray before breaking into bite-sized crackers, or the size of your choice. The crackers can be stored in an airtight container at room temperature for up to 10 days.

To assemble the avocado toast, slice the avocado halves thinly. Gently apply pressure on top of each of the avocado halves using the palm of your hand – this will spread the avocado out so that you have overlapping slices. Season with salt and pepper and a sprinkle of chilli flakes, then drizzle with olive oil. Combine the lemon juice and olive oil and use it to dress the rocket.

Toast the sourdough, then place a slice on each plate. Place half an avocado onto each slice of toast and serve with the rocket and crackers.

French Toast with Caramelized Bananas

///

SERVES / 2

TIME TAKEN / 1 hour

3 large eggs
6 tbsp caster sugar
125ml (4fl oz) double cream
125ml (4fl oz) whole milk
2 tsp good-quality vanilla extract
60ml (2fl oz) thick crème fraîche
2 bananas, peeled and halved lengthways
4 thick slices good-quality brioche
2 tbsp rapeseed oil
25g (1oz) unsalted butter
1 recipe quantity Salted Caramel (see page 148)
1 recipe quantity Berry Compote (see page 149),
* or a handful of fresh summer berries if in season*
icing sugar, for dusting

Crack the eggs into a large mixing bowl and whisk briefly. Add 2 tablespoons of the sugar, the double cream, milk and 1 teaspoon of the vanilla and whisk again for 2–3 minutes until all the ingredients are completely incorporated.

In a bowl, gently fold the remaining 1 teaspoon vanilla extract with the crème fraîche – don't over mix as you want the crème fraîche to be nice and thick. Keep in the fridge until needed.

Put the egg mixture in a deep, flat dish (a baking dish will work) that will fit two slices of the brioche in side by side.

Place the bananas, cut side up, on a baking tray. Cover each half of the banana with 1 tablespoon of the remaining sugar. Caramelise the sugar on the bananas with a blow torch, if you have one. Take care not to hold the blow torch too close to the bananas, or they will burn. If you don't have a blow torch, serve the banana raw.

Preheat the oven to 100°C fan/120°C/250°F/gas 1 and line a baking tray with parchment.

Soak 2 slices of brioche at a time in the batter, making sure the slices are completely soaked by the batter.

Heat a large heavy-based non stick frying pan over a medium heat and add a tablespoon of oil. Remove the soaked brioche slices from the egg mix and carefully shake off excess batter, being careful not to break the brioche. Place the slices in the frying pan and cook for 2–3 minutes, until the undersides of the slices are golden. Add half the butter to the pan and let it melt, then turn the brioche over. Cook the other side of the slices for a further 2 minutes, until golden in colour and the toast is firm to the touch. Place the slices on the prepared baking tray and keep warm in preheated oven. Wipe out the pan with kitchen roll, so that you have a clean pan, then repeat the process to soak and cook the remaining two slices.

Meanwhile, in a pan set over a low heat, gently warm the salted caramel.

To assemble, cut two of the brioche slices in half at an angle, then transfer them to two serving plates, putting two triangles of toast onto each one. Spoon 1 generous tablespoon of vanilla crème fraiche on top of each triangle of French toast, then top with 1 teaspoon of the berry compote. Gently lay half a caramelised banana on top of the berry compote, then drizzle with the salted caramel. Cut the remaining two brioche slices diagonally in half, and place them on top of the banana to make a sandwich on each plate. Dust the toast with icing sugar and serve.

Chilli Crab on Toast with Salted Black Bean and Shrimp Dressing

//

There's a few key ingredient notes to really get the most from this dish. Use fresh crabmeat from the fishmonger if you can, because the taste and texture will be noticeably superior – and worth the extra cost. Most supermarkets will sell crabmeat that has been previously frozen – if you can't find anything else, this is fine, but fresh is the ideal. You can find fermented black beans in the dry food aisle of good Oriental supermarkets. Be sure to rinse them under water before using otherwise they'll be very salty! You will find the dried shrimp in the same shop

SERVES / 2

TIME TAKEN / 30 minutes

100g (3½oz) fresh white crabmeat
1–2 fresh red chillies, deseeded and finely chopped
2 spring onions, finely sliced
zest of 1 lemon
100g (3½oz) samphire
2 Son-in-law Eggs (see page 17)
25g (1oz) butter
2 slices of sourdough bread
sea salt and black pepper
lemon wedges, to serve

FOR THE SALTED BLACK BEAN AND SHRIMP DRESSING
50g (1¾oz) fermented black beans (see above)
50g (1¾oz) dried shrimps
3½ tbsp olive oil
juice of 1 lemon
1 handful of fresh coriander, chopped, plus a few fresh sprigs to serve

Start with the dressing. Soak the fermented black beans in water for about 15 minutes. Place the dried shrimps in a bowl and cover with hot (not boiling) water. Leave to soak for about 15 minutes until the shrimps have doubled in size and are soft to touch.

Meanwhile, prepare the chilli crab. Using your fingers, gently pick through all of the crabmeat to make sure there are no shell fragments in it – this will have been done by the fishmonger, but some pieces may have been missed, so it's worth doing this slightly fiddly step. Tip the crabmeat into a bowl and add the chilli, spring onions and lemon zest. Season with salt and pepper and mix until combined. Cover and store in the fridge until needed.

Once the beans have had their soaking time, rinse them and pat dry with kitchen paper. Drain the shrimps and pat dry with kitchen paper also.

Whisk the olive oil and lemon juice together in a bowl. Add the coriander along with the shrimps and black beans and gently mix together. Set aside until needed.

Bring a pan of water to the boil, add the samphire and blanch for about 30 seconds. Drain the samphire, refresh under cold water, and pat dry with a clean tea towel.

Prepare the son-in-law eggs following the instructions on page 17.

Melt the butter in a frying pan over a medium heat and gently sauté the samphire for a minute until warmed through.

Toast the sourdough bread and arrange on two plates. Place half of the warm samphire on top of each slice of toast and place the chilli crab mixture on top. Spoon the black bean and dried shrimp dressing over the crab. Cut the son-in-law eggs in half and arrange on top of the chilli crab. Garnish with some fresh coriander and serve with a wedge of fresh lemon.

Chicken, Bacon Jam
and Cheddar Toasted Sandwich

//

1 tsp peppercorns
2 garlic cloves, crushed
a few sprigs each of rosemary, thyme and parsley
2 bay leaves
1 carrot, roughly chopped
4 spring onions, roughly chopped
2 free-range or organic chicken breasts, skin on
4 slices sourdough bread
softened butter, for spreading
4 heaped tbsp Bacon Jam (see page 137)
150g (5½oz) mature Cheddar cheese, grated,
plus an optional extra 75g (2½oz) for a cheesy crust

In a small pan large enough to fit the chicken breasts snugly, add the peppercorns, garlic, herbs, bay leaves, carrot, spring onions and 500ml (17fl oz) water. Bring to the boil and simmer for 15 minutes until the water has been infused.

Gently add the chicken to the pan and bring back to the boil. Cover, reduce the heat, and simmer for 10 minutes. Remove from the heat and leave the chicken in the pan to continue cooking in the residual heat while the broth cools down. Once cool, remove the chicken from the broth, it should be cooked through but do check by piercing with a knife and giving it a gentle press – the juices should run clear. Refrigerate until needed.

Arrange your sourdough slices on a chopping board. Spread the outer side of each slice with butter. Take two slices and spread two tablespoons of bacon jam on the non-buttered side of each.

Cut both chicken breasts into thin slices, cutting at an angle across the breast. Arrange the slices on top of the bacon jam, and cover with the grated Cheddar. Place the other slices of bread on top, buttered side up, so you've got two sandwiches ready for toasting.

Heat a large non-stick frying pan over a medium heat. Place both sandwiches in the pan (if they fit, otherwise do one at a time), and cover with a lid. Cook for a few minutes until the underside of the sandwich is golden – check by lifting one with a spatula. Carefully turn the sandwiches over with the spatula. Cover again with the lid and cook for a few minutes until almost done.

For the cheesy crust (why would you not), carefully lift each sandwich in turn with the spatula and sprinkle half of the extra Cheddar into the pan underneath. Try to cover the same area as the sandwich otherwise you'll have wasted cheese. Gently lower the sandwiches back down on top of the cheese and cook for 1–2 minutes until you hear the sizzling of the cheese stop. Wait a few more seconds and then remove the sandwiches from the pan. Slice in half and serve.

Salt Beef, Swiss Cheese and Pickled Cucumber Toastie with Rosemary Crisps

//

Modelled on the classic Reuben,
this has always been one of our
bestsellers. We normally make our
aioli from scratch (see page 150), but
any good quality mayonnaise will
serve as a convenient time-saver to
speed up the process.

SERVES / 2

TIME TAKEN / 30 minutes,
plus overnight pickling

4 slices sourdough bread
softened butter, for spreading
300g (10½oz) Salt Beef (see opposite),
 finely sliced
4 slices Swiss cheese, such as
 Gruyère, Emmental or Jarlsberg

FOR THE PICKLED CUCUMBER

2 cucumbers, peeled and thinly sliced
2 tsp sea salt
200ml (7fl oz) white wine vinegar
125g (4½oz) caster sugar
2 tsp coriander seeds
2 bay leaves
a few sprigs of dill, finely chopped

FOR THE MUSTARD AIOLI

5 tbsp good-quality mayonnaise
1 garlic clove, crushed
1 tsp wholegrain mustard
1 tsp Dijon mustard
juice of ½ lemon

First make the pickled cucumber. Place them in a colander and sprinkle over the salt. Give the cucumber slices a quick massage with your hands to make sure all of the cucumber is coated. Place the colander over the sink and leave to drain for 45 minutes.

Place the vinegar, sugar, coriander seeds and bay leaves in a small pan and bring to the boil. Stir until the sugar has dissolved, then remove from the heat. Strain the liquid to remove the whole spices, and once cool enough, place in the fridge to chill.

Rinse the cucumber slices to remove any remaining salt. Pack them into a sterilised jar (see page 128) and pour over the chilled vinegar liquid. Cover and refrigerate for at least 24 hours.

Make the mustard aioli by combining all of the ingredients in a bowl. If you like more of a kick, add more mustard.

To assemble the sandwiches, arrange your sourdough slices on a chopping board. Spread the outer side of each slice with butter. Take two slices and spread two tablespoons of mustard aioli on the non-buttered side of each. Arrange half the salt beef, 2 cheese slices and some pickled cucumber on top of the mustard aioli covered slices. Close the sandwiches with the two remaining slices, butter sides facing out.

Heat a large non-stick frying pan over a medium heat. Place both sandwiches in the pan (if they fit, otherwise do one at a time), and cover with a lid. Cook for a few minutes until the underside of the sandwich is golden – check by lifting one gingerly with a spatula.

Carefully turn the sandwiches over with the spatula. Cover again with the lid and cook for a few minutes until golden and the cheese is melting.

Remove from the heat, cut in half, and serve.

Salt Beef

//

MAKES / 2kg (4lb 8oz)

TIME TAKEN / 8 hours,
plus brining time

FOR THE BRINE

275g (9¾oz) soft light brown sugar
350g (12oz) sea salt
2 tsp black peppercorns
½ tbsp juniper berries
4 cloves
4 bay leaves
4 sprigs of thyme
55g (2oz) saltpetre

FOR THE BEEF

2kg (4lb 8oz) rolled beef brisket
1 large carrot, roughly chopped
1 onion, roughly chopped
1 celery stick, roughly chopped
1 leek, cut into large chunks
1 bouquet garni
½ head garlic, cloves peeled

*Salt beef needs seven days to brine, so you'll need to think ahead.
You'll be left with plenty of leftovers, though, perfect for sandwiches
like our salt beef sandwich, opposite. You can ask your butcher to roll
the meat, so it is easier to brine and then cook, but flat is just fine. The
salt beef can also be bought already salted from an artisan butcher to
avoid the seven day process but it is fun to experiment, and smoked
salmon can also be used instead of salt beef. Saltpetre is needed to
give the salt beef its characteristic pink-red colour. The beef is pretty
drab without it, so we do advise using it.*

Place all the ingredients for the brine in a large pan and add
2.5 litres (4½ pints) water. Bring it all to the boil, then let it boil
for a couple of minutes, stirring until the salt and sugar have
dissolved. Remove the pan from the heat and allow the brine to
cool completely.

Pierce the brisket all over with a skewer. Place it in a large
plastic container and pour over the brine until the meat is totally
submerged. You may need to weigh down the meat in order to
keep it submerged, so a couple of heavy bottles or jars placed
directly on top of the meat will do. Leave in a very cool place –
a fridge or the coldest room in your home – for a week.

Remove the beef from the brine and rinse it. Place it in a large
pan with the vegetables, bouquet garni and garlic and cover
with cold water. Bring the water to a boil, then reduce the heat
to a simmer, cover loosely and very gently poach the brisket for
5–7 hours, until the meat is tender and can be torn easily. Check
on it occasionally and add a splash of water if the water is getting
low. Remove from the heat and leave the brisket in the stock water
to cool completely.

Remove the brisket from the brine, wrap it in cling film and store
in the fridge for up to 10 days.

The Sunday BLT

//

It may seem slightly audacious including a recipe for what is one of the most classic sandwiches of all time, but we maintain that this is one of the best you'll ever have. The secret? The quality of the ingredients, and cooking the bacon to a perfect crispness, which contrasts sublimely with the soft farmhouse bread and other ingredients.

SERVES / 2

TIME TAKEN / 30 minutes

12 slices dry cured streaky bacon
4 thick slices fresh soft white bread (farmhouse or bloomer is perfect)
4 tbsp good-quality mayonnaise (or Aioli, see page 150)
1 baby gem lettuce, leaves separated
2 punnets mustard cress
2 ripe plum tomatoes, sliced
1 avocado, peeled, stoned and finely sliced
6 slices mature Cheddar cheese (about 100g / 3½oz)
sea salt and black pepper

Preheat the oven to 180°C fan/200°C/400°F/ gas 6 and line a baking tray with parchment.

Lay the bacon on the tray in a single layer, making sure it's not overlapping. Cook in the oven for around 15 minutes, or until it is slightly crispy.

Spread some of the bacon fat from the baking tray (there will be plenty, trust us) on one side of each slice of bread.

Heat a large frying pan over a medium heat and place the bread in it, fat side down. Heat for 1–2 minutes until the bread is slightly crispy and golden brown, then remove from the heat.

Spread the non-crispy side of each slice of bread with a thick layer of mayonnaise; the guiding principle here is that if you think you've used enough, you haven't, so use some more.

Now assemble your sandwiches. Taking two slices of bread as the bases, arrange half the lettuce leaves on each slice, then add a generous amount of cress. Place the sliced tomatoes on top of the cress, and lightly season with salt and pepper. Arrange the avocado on top, followed by the cheese. Top with the crispy bacon, and finish with the other slice of bread, pressing down lightly to help it hold together. Slice in half, take to a cosy spot, and enjoy

Kimchi and Halloumi Toasties

//

SERVES / 2

TIME TAKEN / 50 minutes

100g (3½oz) plain flour
1 egg
1 handful of fresh parsley, chopped
zest of 1 lemon
150g (5½oz) panko breadcrumbs
6 slices of aubergine, around 1cm (½in) thick
rapeseed oil, for frying
250g (9oz) pack halloumi, cut into 6 slices
olive oil, for brushing
butter, for spreading
4 large slices sourdough bread
6 tbsp Kimchi (see page 150)
1 handful of rocket leaves
olive oil, for dressing
sea salt and black pepper

Preheat the oven to 100°C fan/120°C/250°F/gas 1 and line a baking tray with parchment.

Place the flour in a bowl and season with salt and pepper. Crack the egg into a second bowl and beat it. In a third bowl, mix together the chopped parsley, lemon zest and panko breadcrumbs.

Dip a slice of aubergine into the flour, making sure it is coated on both sides. Shake off the excess and then dip it into the beaten egg mix. Coat on both sides, shake off any hanging-on drips, and finally dip into the panko crumb mixture, ensuring it is well coated all over. Place on a plate and repeat the process with the remaining aubergine slices.

Pour rapeseed oil to a depth of 1cm (½in) in a large frying pan and set over a medium heat. Test the oil's temperature by gently dropping in a small piece of bread; at the right temperature, it will sizzle and start to brown, but not blacken. If the oil is too hot, remove the pan from the heat and allow to cool until you pass the golden bread test.

Gently place the crumbed aubergine slices in the hot oil and cook for 5–6 minutes, turning halfway through, until both sides are golden brown. You may need to do this in two batches if your pan is not big enough. When the aubergine slices are ready, place them on kitchen paper to absorb the excess oil, then transfer them to the oven to keep warm whilst cooking the halloumi.

Remove the aubergine oil from the frying pan and wipe the pan clean. Return the pan to the hob over a medium-high heat. Brush each slice of halloumi with some olive oil, then fry them for about 2 minutes on each side until golden brown. Transfer the halloumi to the oven to keep warm with the aubergine.

Butter both sides of all the bread slices, then spread 3 tablespoons kimchi evenly across two slices of the bread. Lay the crispy aubergine on top of the kimchi, then add 3 slices of halloumi on top of the aubergine. Close the sandwiches with the remaining slices of sourdough, and gently press down.

Put the large frying pan back over the heat and carefully place a sandwich in the pan. Allow to get golden brown on the bottom, 3–4 minutes, before turning over and browning on the other side. Once the sandwich is golden brown on both sides and you can see the halloumi and kimchi merge, remove the sandwich from the pan onto a chopping board, cut in half and repeat with the other sandwich. Lightly dress the rocket with the olive oil and serve alongside the sandwiches.

Waffles, Pancakes and Fritters

Buttermilk Waffles with Cured Salmon and Wasabi Cream Cheese

//

For the salmon, ask your fishmonger for a thick piece from the middle of the fish – this will help even curing all over. Remove the brown, oily meat as well. You can cure the salmon in a zipper bag or plastic container – just don't use anything metal.

2 Poached Eggs (see page 14)
½ avocado, peeled, stoned and sliced
1 spring onion, finely sliced
1 tsp black sesame seeds
a few sprigs fresh coriander
olive oil, to drizzle

FOR THE CURED SALMON

250ml (9fl oz) light soy sauce
250ml (9fl oz) maple syrup
50g (1¾oz) sea salt
half a bunch of fresh coriander,
   chopped (leaves and stalks)
5cm (2in) piece of fresh ginger, peeled
   and grated
2 garlic cloves, finely sliced
1 green chilli, chopped
juice and zest of 1 lime
500g (1lb 2oz) salmon fillet, bones
   and brown meat removed

FOR THE WASABI CREAM CHEESE

2 heaped tbsp full-fat cream cheese
1 tsp wasabi paste
juice of 1 lime

FOR THE WAFFLES

150g (5½oz) plain flour
1 tsp baking powder
a pinch of sea salt
50g (1¾oz) butter, melted
250ml (9fl oz) buttermilk
2 eggs, beaten
oil spray, for greasing

For the salmon, whisk together the soy sauce, maple syrup and salt in a bowl until the salt has dissolved. Add the coriander, ginger, garlic, chilli and lime juice and zest, and mix well. Place the salmon in a large zipper food storage bag or plastic container (don't use anything metal as it will affect the taste) and pour over the curing marinade. Make sure the salmon is submerged in the marinade. Cover (or zip the bag shut) and place in the fridge for 24 hours.

Remove the salmon from the fridge and rinse under cold water to remove the marinade. The salmon will have taken on a tinge of colour from the fragrant soy-based cure. Pat the fillet dry. Using a sharp knife, slice the salmon at a 45-degree angle into 5mm (¼in) slices. Lay the slices flat on a plate and tightly cover with cling film so that it is airtight. Refrigerate until needed.

Combine all the ingredients for the wasabi cream cheese in a small bowl. Cover and refrigerate until needed.

Prepare the waffle mix by combining the flour, baking powder and salt in a bowl. Mix the wet ingredients in a separate bowl, then add the wet to the dry and whisk together gently until the batter is smooth, taking care not to overbeat.

Heat up the waffle machine and spray with oil. Pour a ladleful of waffle batter into the machine and cook for 3–4 minutes or until golden brown and crispy on the outside. Repeat so you have two waffles. While the waffles are cooking, poach the eggs (see page 14).

Assemble each serving plate by placing a few slices of cured salmon across one half of each waffle. Add a neatly heaped tablespoon of wasabi cream cheese then place the poached egg on an empty quarter of the waffle with the sliced avocado on the remaining quarter. Garnish with the spring onion, black sesame seeds and a few sprigs of coriander, and finish off with a drizzle of olive oil. Serve and enjoy.

Pulled Pork on Waffle Benedict

//

*There's quite a lot of time and effort
that goes into this dish but it's well worth
every second. Pulled pork and waffles
is a big hitter amongst brunch lovers,
and replacing the muffin – traditionally
used in a benedict – with a waffle was
a game changer for us, as is the yuzu
hollandaise, which cuts through the salty
pork. If you have an early breakfast, the
pork can be cooked the day before and
reheated, covered with foil, in the oven.*

SERVES / 2

TIME TAKEN / 30 minutes

FOR THE PULLED PORK

a pinch of sweet smoked paprika
a pinch of ground cumin
1 garlic clove, crushed
6 sprigs fresh thyme
1 tbsp olive oil
400g (14oz) lean pork shoulder
sea salt and black pepper

FOR THE WAFFLES

2 eggs
250ml (9fl oz) buttermilk
50g (1¾oz) butter, melted and
  cooled slightly
150g (5½oz) plain flour
1 tsp baking powder

TO SERVE

4 Poached Eggs (see page 14)
Yuzu Hollandaise (see page 157)
30g (1¼oz) watercress
1 tbsp olive oil
2 lime wedges
1 avocado, peeled, stoned and sliced

Preheat the oven to 130°C fan/150°C/300°F/gas 2.

In a small bowl, mix together the smoked paprika, cumin, garlic, thyme and olive oil and season with salt and pepper. Pour the marinade over the pork shoulder.

Heat a non-stick frying pan over a medium heat and seal the pork shoulder on each side for 2 minutes.

Place the pork into a small 5cm (2in) deep oven tray, add 125ml (4½fl oz) water and cover with foil. Roast for 2–3 hours until the meat is tender and can be pulled apart. Once cooked, remove from the oven and allow to rest for 10 minutes. When rested, carefully pull the meat into large pieces using a pair of tongs and a fork. Cover with foil and keep warm in a low oven while you prepare the waffles.

Prepare the waffle mix by combining the flour, baking powder and salt in a bowl. Mix the wet ingredients in a separate bowl, then add the wet to the dry and whisk together gently until the batter is smooth, taking care not to overbeat.

Heat up the waffle machine. Scoop a ladleful of the batter into the machine, close the lid and cook for around 5–6 minutes. The waffle should be golden crisp on both sides and super fluffy in the middle when ready.

While the waffles are cooking, poach the eggs. Place a waffle on each plate and divide the pulled pork between each one. Place 2 eggs per person on top of the pork, then drizzle with the yuzu hollandaise. Dress the watercress with the olive oil and pile it on top of the waffles. Serve with lime wedges and sliced avocado.

Roasted Fruit Waffle with Almond Brittle

//

SERVES / 2

TIME TAKEN / 1 hour

2 ripe peaches, 1 halved
2 ripe nectarines, 1 halved
2 plums, 1 halved
2 tbsp caster sugar
½ vanilla pod, split

FOR THE ALMOND BRITTLE

50g (1¾oz) flaked almonds
25g (1oz) unsalted butter
50g (1¾oz) caster sugar

FOR THE WAFFLES

2 eggs
250ml (9fl oz) buttermilk
50g (1¾oz) butter, melted and
cooled slightly
150g (5½oz) plain flour
1 tsp caster sugar
1 tsp baking powder

FOR THE VANILLA
MASCARPONE

1 tsp vanilla extract
2 heaped tablespoons
Mascarpone cheese
1 tsp caster sugar

TO SERVE

1 handful of blackberries
4 fresh mint leaves,
finely chopped

Place the halved peach, nectarine and plum in a small pan with enough water to cover. Bring to the boil over a high heat and cook for 10–12 minutes until the fruit has started to break down and the water has slightly reduced. Remove from the heat and strain using a sieve.

Discard the pulp and put the juice back into the pan. Add the sugar and vanilla, place back over a medium heat and cook for a further 8–10 minutes until reduced, rose amber in colour and the syrup lightly coats the back of a tablespoon. Remove from the heat and allow to cool for 15 minutes.

Cut the remaining fruit into wedges, remove the stones and place in a mixing bowl. Pour the cooled syrup over the fruit and gently fold so that the syrup completely coats it. Set aside until needed.

To make the almond brittle, line a baking tray with parchment and spread the flaked almonds across the tray. Put the butter, caster sugar and 2 tablespoons water into a non-stick frying pan and heat gently over a low heat, until the sugar has dissolved. Increase the heat to medium and boil for 4–5 minutes, until it starts to turn a light golden brown, stirring often as some parts of the pan may caramelize quicker than others.

Carefully pour the hot caramel over the almonds and allow to cool completely. Once cold, break the almond brittle into chunks. Can be stored in an airtight container for 2 days at ambient temperature and it also freezes really well.

Prepare the waffle mix by combining the flour, baking powder and sugar in a bowl. Mix the wet ingredients in a separate bowl, then add the wet to the dry and whisk together gently until the batter is smooth, taking care not to overbeat.

Heat up the waffle machine. Pour a ladleful of batter into the machine, close the lid and cook for 5–6 minutes. The waffle should be crisp on both sides and super fluffy in the middle when ready.

Stir together all the ingredients for the vanilla mascarpone in a small bowl.

Place a waffle onto each of the serving plates. Spoon the vanilla mascarpone and fruit over both waffles then pour over the syrup. Scatter with the blackberries, chopped mint and shards of almond brittle.

Buttermilk Pancakes

//

A large flat top grill in a professional kitchen is perfect for cooking lots of pancakes at the same time. We don't have this luxury at home, so we use two large non-stick frying pans instead. Alternatively, cook the pancakes in batches and keep them warm in the oven whilst you make more. In the summer months, fresh berries make a delicious alternative to the compote.

SERVES / 4

TIME TAKEN / 50 minutes

125g (4½oz) unsalted butter
450g (1lb) self-raising flour
1 tbsp baking powder
170g (6oz) caster sugar
3 large eggs
560ml (19¼fl oz) buttermilk
rapeseed oil, for greasing

TO SERVE
16 rashers good-quality dry-cured
  streaky bacon
4 tbsp Berry Compote (see page 149)
4 slices Honeycomb Butter
  (see page 154)
good-quality maple syrup, to drizzle

Preheat the oven to 170°C fan/190°C/375°F/gas 5. Place the bacon on a baking tray and cook in the oven until crispy. Place on kitchen paper, then set aside.

While the bacon is cooking, start the pancake batter. Melt the butter gently in a small pan over a low heat. Set aside to cool for 10 minutes. Once the bacon is cooked, lower the oven temperature to 100°C fan/120°C/250°F/gas 1 and line another baking tray with parchment.

Sift the flour and baking powder into a bowl, then mix in the sugar. Set aside.

Crack the eggs into a large mixing bowl and beat together, then whisk in the buttermilk until combined. Now, fold the melted butter into the egg mixture using a spatula. Once the butter is incorporated, add the flour mix and gently fold together until you have a thick pancake batter, being careful not to over mix – a few lumps here or there is not a bad thing. Set the batter aside for 10 minutes to settle before cooking.

Place 2 large non-stick frying pans over a low heat and brush with oil just to coat. Once the pans are hot, spoon 4 generous tablespoons of the pancake batter into each pan, so you are simultaneously cooking 8 pancakes. Cook the pancakes gently for 5–6 minutes, until set and golden on the bottom. Flip them over and cook for a further 4–5 minutes, until golden on the bottom again and doubled in size.

Once the first 8 pancakes are almost cooked, transfer them to the prepared baking tray and put them in the oven to keep warm and fluffy while you cook the rest. Once all the pancakes are cooked it's time to assemble the dish.

Stack 4 pancakes on each of 4 serving plates. Spoon a tablespoon of berry compote onto the top of each stack. Criss-cross 4 pieces of bacon on top of the compote, then balance a slice of the honeycomb butter on top. Drizzle with the maple syrup, go forth and conquer.

Spinach, Pea and Parmesan Pancakes

//

SERVES / 2

TIME TAKEN / 1 hour

25g (1oz) butter, plus extra for
  cooking the pancakes
60g (2oz) spinach, washed and dried
100ml (3½fl oz) milk
100g (3½oz) boiled or steamed peas
6 large mint leaves
200g (7oz) self-raising flour
1 tsp baking powder
3 eggs
50g (1¾oz) Parmesan cheese, grated

FOR THE ROASTED SQUASH

1 small onion squash
2 tbsp olive oil
zest of 1 lemon

FOR THE CAULIFLOWER PURÉE

½ small cauliflower
1 garlic clove
1 tbsp cream cheese
a pinch of freshly grated nutmeg

FOR THE PESTO

1 good handful of basil
1 good handful of parsley
2 garlic cloves
50g (1¾oz) pine nuts
120ml (4oz) olive oil, plus extra for
  storing
50g (1¾oz) Parmesan cheese, grated
sea salt and black pepper

TO SERVE

2 Poached Eggs (see page 14)
rocket leaves
Parmesan shavings

Onion squash is one of the earliest squashes of the season. Its soft skin needs no peeling, and it has a delicious sweetness which is enhanced through roasting, but butternut squash makes a good substitute. And both look great against the vibrant green pancakes.

First, make the pesto. Put the basil, parsley, garlic and half the pine nuts into the bowl of a food processor and blitz until it's combined and smooth (you can also use a stick blender). While the processor is still running, pour in the olive oil in a steady stream. Stop the machine and scrape down the sides. Transfer the pesto to a bowl and fold in the remaining pine nuts and the Parmesan. Add salt and pepper to taste. Store the pesto in a jar in the fridge, topped with a layer of olive oil to seal, for up to 5 days.

Next, prepare the onion squash. Preheat the oven to 170°C fan/190°C/375°F/gas 5. Slice the squash in half and scoop out the seeds, then cut it into 2.5cm (1in) thick slices. Place the slices in a bowl and drizzle with the olive oil. Add the lemon zest and seasoning and mix it all together, massaging into the squash. Transfer the slices to a roasting dish and roast in the preheated oven for 25 minutes until soft and caramelising at the edges.

While the squash is cooking, prepare the cauliflower purée. Cut the cauliflower in half so you have two pieces. Cut out the core and discard, then break the rest into large florets. Bring a pan of salted water to the boil and add the florets and garlic. Cook for around 15 minutes until tender.

Drain off the water and transfer the cauliflower and garlic to a food processor. Add the cream cheese, a pinch of grated nutmeg and salt and pepper to taste and blitz until smooth and creamy. Transfer to a small pan so you can warm it gently before serving.

Now prepare the pancakes. Start by melting the butter in a frying pan over a medium heat. Add the spinach and cook until just wilted. Transfer the cooked spinach to a mixing bowl and add the milk, half the peas and the mint leaves. Purée everything together using a stick blender until smooth. Add the rest of the peas and roughly blitz for another few seconds so that the peas are roughly chopped but there is still some texture in the batter.

Add the flour, baking powder, eggs and Parmesan to the mixture and mix with a wooden spoon until evenly combined. Don't worry if there are still a few lumps in the batter. What will emerge is a rather thick, beautiful, vibrantly green batter. Let it rest for 10 minutes.

Melt a knob of butter in a large non-stick frying pan over a medium heat. Spoon 3 tablespoons of batter per pancake into the pan. Depending on the size of your pan you should be able to cook 2–3 pancakes in one go. Cook the pancakes for 3–4 minutes on each side until they are golden green–brown. Repeat until you have 6 pancakes, adding a little more butter to the pan when needed.

Warm the cauliflower purée gently in the pan and spread 3 tablespoons on each plate. Layer with a stack of three pancakes, a couple of slices of roast squash and a poached egg. Garnish with a few rocket leaves and some Parmesan shavings. Finish off with a good drizzle of the pesto and serve.

TIP /

You can prepare the pesto in advance and store it in the fridge, ready to use for this dish or any other recipe.

Pork Belly, Crispy Spring Onion Pancakes and Kimchi Scrambled Eggs

//

SERVES / 2

TIME TAKEN / 4 hours, plus marinating time

500g (1lb 2oz) boneless belly of pork, skin on

1 tbsp table salt

2 tbsp vegetable oil

1 potato, to make a 'stand'

2 Crispy Spring Onion Pancakes (see page 101)

4 eggs

a knob of butter

4 tbsp Kimchi (see page 150)

¼ cucumber, peeled and sliced

2 tbsp kecap manis

Lime wedges, to serve

FOR THE RUB

1 tbsp fennel seeds

2 garlic cloves

2 tsp fresh thyme leaves

zest of 1 lemon

1 tsp sea salt

1 tsp black pepper

2 tbsp vegetable oil

It is important that you buy the pork belly with skin on for that all-important crackling which takes this dish to another level. The recipe probably makes more pork belly than you need, but you can use it for other things, and it will keep in the fridge for up to 3 days. If you're planning ahead, it's better to do the preparation of the pork a day or two in advance, as there are a few hours of cooking and preparation involved. Make sure the skin is dry to ensure maximum crispiness and that enticing crackling. This might look like a complicated dish, but once you have prepared the pork it's about assembling the three components of pork, spring onion pancakes and scrambled eggs.

Start by making the rub. In a frying pan, toast the fennel seeds for a minute over a medium heat until they start to release their aroma. Transfer to a pestle and mortar and crush until well ground. Add the garlic to the mortar and continue crushing until smooth. Add the remaining rub ingredients and combine into a paste.

Using a sharp knife, score the pork belly skin in criss-cross patterns along its length. Rub the table salt into the skin, making sure to get it into the scores. Turn the belly over, so it's flesh side up, and massage the paste into the flesh until it is well covered. Place the pork belly in a dish, skin side up, cover with cling film and leave to marinate in the fridge for a few hours.

Preheat the oven to 220°C fan/240°C/475°F/gas 9. Remove the pork belly from the fridge. You'll find that the salt will have drawn out moisture from the skin, making it quite wet. For the perfect crackling, the skin needs to be as dry as possible, so pat dry using kitchen paper, then rub the vegetable oil evenly all over the skin.

Take a deep-sided roasting dish that can snugly accommodate the pork belly. While the pork is cooking it will release a lot of fat, which will collect in the bottom of the dish. To prevent the underside of the belly getting soggy from the fat, we place it on little 'stands' to keep it elevated. You can do this by cutting a potato into 1cm (½in) slices and placing it in the dish. Rest the pork on top, skin side up, and place in the oven. (These potato 'legs' will be delicious once the pork is done!)

Roast the pork in the preheated oven for about 25 minutes, until the skin is crispy and golden. Reduce the heat to 160°C fan/180°C/350°F/gas 4 and roast for a further 2½ hours, or until the flesh is tender and easy to tear with the tip of a knife. Remove the pork from the oven and allow to cool to room temperature. Once cool, wrap tightly in cling film and refrigerate for at least 2 hours or overnight.

Just before you start preparing the rest of the dish, remove the pork from the fridge and unwrap the cling film. Using a sharp knife, trim the edges so you have a neat rectangle, then cut in half.

Start preparing the remaining elements of the dish. Preheat the oven to 170°C fan/190°C/375°F/gas 5. Place the two pieces of pork belly on a roasting tray and re-heat in the oven for 15 minutes, or until they are warmed through.

Meanwhile, cook the spring onion pancakes as per the recipe on page 101. Keep these warm in the oven with the pork.

Crack the eggs into a bowl and beat together lightly with a pinch of salt. In a heavy-based pan, heat the knob of butter over a medium heat. Add the eggs and scramble until almost done to your liking. Add the kimchi and fold it into the eggs. Remove from the heat.

To serve, place a spring onion pancake on each plate. Top with the kimchi scrambled eggs, a piece of pork belly, cucumber and the lime wedges, and drizzle with kecap manis.

Cauliflower Hotcakes with Cherry Tomato, Broad Bean and Avocado Salsa

//

Our cauliflower hotcakes are best served immediately, when still crisp and hot from the pan. They are great as an afternoon snack too. The hotcakes and the bacon take around the same time to cook, so try to get them cooking at the same time to make it easier when assembling.

SERVES / 4

TIME TAKEN / 45 minutes

½ *small cauliflower, cut into small florets*
125g (4½oz) *self-raising flour*
2 *large eggs, lightly beaten*
½ *red onion, finely diced*
2 *garlic cloves, finely chopped*
½ *red chilli, deseeded and finely diced*
½ *bunch of fresh coriander, chopped*
1½ *tsp ground cumin*
½ *tsp ground turmeric*
1 *tsp sea salt*
1 *tsp black pepper*
12 *slices dry-cured streaky bacon*
3 *tbsp rapeseed oil, plus extra if needed*
4 *Poached Eggs (see page 14)*
4 *tbsp Tahini Lemon Yoghurt (see page 144)*
Cherry Tomato, Broad Bean and Avocado Salsa (see page 145)
olive oil, to drizzle

Bring a pan of salted water to the boil, add the cauliflower and blanch for 3 minutes. Fish out with a slotted spoon and drain in a colander, transfer to a plate and allow to cool for 15 minutes.

While the cauliflower is cooling, sift the flour into a mixing bowl and whisk in the eggs to create a thick batter. Add the onion, garlic, chilli, coriander, cumin, turmeric and the salt and pepper. Mix well using a plastic spatula.

Break the cauliflower pieces into smaller florets so that the hotcakes aren't too chunky. Add the florets to the batter and mix well until fully incorporated – you should have a thick stiff batter.

Preheat the grill to high. Line a tray with kitchen paper to drain the fritters on once cooked.

Lay the bacon onto a non-stick baking tray and grill until the fat is almost crispy, or to your desired taste.

Meanwhile, heat a large heavy-based non-stick frying pan over a medium heat. Add 3 tablespoons of rapeseed oil to the pan and allow to heat for a minute or so. Put 4 heaped tablespoons of the hotcake mix into the pan, spacing them out, and allow to fry for 3–4 minutes before flipping over and cooking for a further 2–3 minutes until crisp and golden brown. Remove from the pan and drain on kitchen paper. Repeat to cook another two batches of the hotcakes, adding a little more oil if needed.

Prepare the poached eggs as per the recipe on page 14.

To assemble, spread a generous tablespoon of tahini lemon yoghurt in the centre of each plate and place 3 hotcakes onto the plate. Add 2 tablespoons of the salsa and 3 slices of bacon. Finish each plate with a poached egg and a drizzle of olive oil.

Courgette Fritters with Halloumi, Dukkah and Mint Yoghurt

//

This is one of our most photographed dishes. There are lots of elements and it's all about timing so you'll need to be quick once you're ready to assemble the dish! No pressure. Nail it and you'll be a brunch legend!

SERVES / 2

TIME TAKEN / 1½ hours

125g (4½oz) block halloumi cheese
olive oil, for brushing
2 courgettes
2 large eggs
75g (2½oz) plain flour
rapeseed oil, for frying
2 Poached Eggs (see page 14)

FOR THE COURGETTE CRUST
75g (2½oz) panko breadcrumbs
½ tsp dried chilli flakes
½ small bunch chopped coriander, plus extra sprigs to garnish
1 garlic clove, finely chopped
1 tsp ground white pepper
25g (1oz) plain flour
15g (½oz) cornflour
1 tsp sea salt
zest of ½ lemon
½ tsp onion powder

TO SERVE
60g (2oz) baby mixed salad leaves (such as rocket, baby spinach, watercress, ruby chard)
1 tbsp olive oil
4 tbsp Dukkah (see page 141)
Parmesan cheese, shaved
4 tbsp Mint Yoghurt (see page 142)
1 avocado, peeled, pitted and sliced
2 tsp Harissa (see page 140)
sea salt and black pepper

Preheat the oven to 130°C fan/150°C/300°F/gas 2 and line a baking tray with parchment.

Make the breadcrumb crust for the courgettes. In a large bowl, toss all the ingredients together until thoroughly mixed.

Cut the halloumi into 2 thick slices and brush with olive oil. Set aside.

Wash the courgettes and slice off the ends. Cut them both into quarters lengthways, so you have 8 long pieces of courgette.

Crack the eggs into a deep dish large enough to accommodate the courgette strips. Beat them and season with salt and pepper.

Put the flour in a dish of a similar size to the one containing the eggs, making sure the courgette strips will fit. Put the breadcrumb crust mix in a third dish – again this needs to fit the courgettes.

Dip the courgette quarters into the flour, then into the beaten egg mixture and, lastly, into the breadcrumb mix. Once fully coated, place the strips on the prepared baking tray, leaving space between them so they don't stick together.

Use a large, deep non-stick frying pan and add enough rapeseed oil to fill the pan to a depth of 4cm (1½in). Carefully heat the oil until it reaches 180°C / 350°F on a thermometer. If you don't have a thermometer, you can test whether the oil is hot by cutting a cube of bread and frying until golden – which should only take a few minutes (if the bread darkens too quickly the oil is too hot and the temperature needs to be lowered).

Once the oil is ready, place 4 courgette strips into the pan and cook until golden and crisp, about

5–7 minutes, turning regularly with a slotted spoon so that they brown evenly. Once cooked, remove from the oil with a slotted spoon and place on to a tray lined with kitchen paper to soak up any excess oil. Repeat with the remaining courgette strips.

Whilst the courgettes are frying, place the halloumi in a separate dry frying pan and cook over a medium heat for 1–2 minutes on each side until golden all over.

Prepare the poached eggs as per the recipe on page 14.

In a bowl, toss the salad leaves with the olive oil, dukkah and Parmesan.

Now assemble the dish. Spread 2 tablespoons of the mint yoghurt in a small circle in the centre of a serving plate. Place half a sliced avocado on top of the yoghurt, slightly to the right, leaving enough space on the left to place a halloumi slice. Add 1 teaspoon of harissa in the middle, sitting on top of the halloumi and avocado.

Next, place two of the courgette fritters on the stack, one on top of the halloumi and the other on top of the avocado. Take two more fritters and place at right angles on top of the fritters on the plate, so that you have a box of courgette fritters surrounding the harissa.

Place a poached egg inside the fritter box on top of the harissa. Finish by placing half of the dressed salad leaves on top of the fritters, covering the poached egg. Repeat the process to build the second dish in the same way.

Garnish both plates with a sprig of coriander, then serve and enjoy.

Salt Beef and Potato Pancakes

//

SERVES / 2

TIME TAKEN / 50 minutes

FOR THE SALT BEEF AND POTATO PANCAKES

2–3 Maris Piper potatoes
  (approximately 300g/10½oz),
  peeled and halved
2 eggs
250ml (9fl oz) buttermilk
150g (5½oz) plain flour
2 tsp baking powder
2 spring onions, finely sliced
2 tsp grated Parmesan cheese
60g (2oz) Cheddar cheese, grated
200g (7oz) Salt Beef (see page 57),
  finely diced
1 tsp wholegrain mustard
1 tsp sea salt
1 tsp black pepper
vegetable oil, for frying

FOR THE HERBED CRÈME FRAÎCHE

4 tbsp crème fraîche
2 tbsp chopped chives
grated zest of 1 lemon

TO SERVE

2 Poached Eggs (see page 14)
Pickled Cucumber (see page 56)
2 tbsp Beetroot and Dill Purée
  (see page 144)
Parmesan cheese, shaved
olive oil

For the pancakes, place the potatoes in a pan of water and bring it to the boil. Cook for 15–20 minutes, or until tender. Drain well and allow to cool slightly in the colander before transferring to a bowl and mashing roughly with a fork. Don't worry about a few lumps – they add texture (which is good). You should have around 250g (9oz) of mashed potato.

In a separate bowl, lightly beat the eggs together with the buttermilk. Add this mixture to the mashed potatoes and gently mix together. Sift in the flour and baking powder and mix again, taking care to not beat it too furiously otherwise the mixture could become too glutinous resulting in chewy pancakes. Add all the remaining pancake ingredients except the vegetable oil and mix together until combined. Cover and leave to rest for 15 minutes.

Preheat the oven to 100°C fan/120°C/250°F/gas 1.

Heat a large non-stick frying pan over a low-medium heat and add enough vegetable oil to coat the base. When the oil is hot, add 3 tablespoons of the batter per pancake – fit in as many as you can into the pan without overcrowding it – and cook for about 2 minutes until the underside is golden and small bubbles appear on the surface. Flip the pancakes over and cook on the other side until golden. Remove from the pan and keep warm in the oven while you cook the rest. You should be able to make 6 pancakes.

Mix together the crème fraîche, chopped chives, lemon zest, and a pinch of salt and pepper in a small bowl.

To serve, spread a couple of tablespoons of the herbed crème fraîche on each of 2 serving plates and place three pancakes on top. Place a poached egg on top of each pancake stack, then add a small handful of the pickled cucumber and a tablespoon of the beetroot and dill purée to each plate. Serve with the shaved Parmesan and finish with a drizzle of olive oil.

Corn Fritters with Avocado and Honey Smoked Salmon

//

SERVES / 2

TIME TAKEN / 45 minutes

3 fresh corn on the cob, corn removed from the husk
2 eggs
150g (5½oz) self-raising flour
3 spring onions, finely sliced
½ red chilli, deseeded and finely diced
½ small bunch coriander, chopped, plus extra to garnish
4 tbsp rapeseed oil, plus extra if needed
butter, for brushing
sea salt and black pepper

TO SERVE
2 tbsp good-quality thick crème fraiche
2 plum vine tomatoes, sliced
1 avocado, halved, stoned and peeled
1 fillet honey smoked salmon (you'll find this in good quality fishmongers)
2 tbsp Roast Corn Salsa (see page 145)
2 tbsp Chilli Jam (see page 136)
olive oil, to drizzle
sea salt and black pepper, to taste

Using a small serrated knife, remove the corn kernels from the cob and set aside.

Crack the eggs into a large mixing bowl and give them a whisk. Add the flour and mix until you have a smooth, thick batter. Add the corn, spring onions, chilli and coriander. Season and mix until well incorporated.

Heat the rapeseed oil in large heavy-based non-stick frying pan over a medium heat. When the oil is hot, add 6 tablespoons of the batter to the pan to make 6 individual fritters. Fry gently for 3–4 minutes until golden brown and crisp before turning over. Cook for a further 3–4 minutes on the other side, adding more oil if necessary. Brush the corn fritters gently with butter to finish.

To assemble, spread 1 tablespoon of crème fraiche on each of 2 serving plates, and top with a sliced tomato and half of the avocado and flaked salmon. Scatter over 1 tablespoon of corn salsa and 1 tablespoon of chilli jam. Add 3 corn fritters to each plate, drizzle with olive oil and garnish with coriander.

Sunday Specialities

Cauliflower Couscous and Cracked Wheat Breakfast Bowl

//

SERVES / 2

TIME TAKEN / 1 hour

1 small sweet potato
50g (1¾oz) cracked wheat
½ small cauliflower (about 200g / 7oz)
50g (1¾oz) kale (leaf removed from the stem)
30g (1¼oz) edamame beans
2 spring onions, finely sliced
½ bunch fresh coriander, shredded
seeds from 1 small pomegranate
4 slices pancetta (sliced or cubed are both fine)
rapeseed oil, for frying
2 eggs
1 avocado, peeled, stoned and cut into wedges

FOR THE MISO DRESSING

1½ tbsp white miso paste
2 tbsp rice wine vinegar
1 tbsp sesame oil
1 tbsp maple syrup
¼ red chilli, deseeded and finely diced

Preheat the oven to 170°C fan/190°C/375°F/gas 5. Place the sweet potato on a baking tray and roast in the oven for about 30 minutes, or until soft to the touch when given a gentle squeeze.

Meanwhile, to make the miso dressing, put all the ingredients into a small mixing bowl and whisk until fully incorporated – the dressing should have a silky finish. Set aside at room temperature.

Bring a small pan of salted water to a boil, add the cracked wheat and cook for 6 minutes, or until tender. Drain and leave in a strainer to cool.

Cut out the core of the cauliflower and discard. Break the rest into large florets. Put the florets in a food processor and pulse in 1-second bursts until broken down into couscous-sized granules. Alternatively, grate the florets using the large holes of a box grater. Transfer to a large mixing bowl.

Bring a small pan of salted water to the boil and add the kale and edamame. Bring the water back to the boil, then blanch for 2 minutes. Remove the vegetables from the heat and refresh in ice water. Drain in a colander, then extract the kale and dry using kitchen paper before finely slicing.

Put the cracked wheat, edamame, kale and cauliflower couscous in a large bowl. Remove the sweet potato from the oven and allow to cool before peeling and discarding the skin. Chop into 1cm (½in) cubes and add to the bowl with the spring onions, coriander and pomegranate seeds. Give the dressing a quick whisk, as it will probably have separated, then add it to the bowl. Mix until everything is evenly coated, then divide the salad into two serving bowls.

Heat a heavy-based frying pan over a low heat and add the pancetta. Cook for around 5 minutes on each side until some of the fat has rendered. Turn the heat up to medium–high and continue to cook until crisp and turning golden. Remove from the pan and keep warm in the oven.

Wipe the frying pan clean and add some rapeseed oil. Crack in the eggs and fry to your liking. Place a fried egg on top of the salad in each serving bowl and add the avocado wedges. Top with the crispy pancetta and serve.

Vegan Falafel and Beetroot Salad Bowl

//

FOR THE HUMMUS

1 x 400g (14 oz) tin chickpeas,
  drained and rinsed
4 tbsp olive oil
2 garlic cloves, crushed
juice of 1 lemon
3 tbsp tahini
1 tsp ground cumin
sea salt and black pepper

FOR THE FALAFEL

1 x 400g (14 oz) tin chickpeas,
  drained and rinsed
½ bunch fresh coriander
  (about 15g / ½ oz), roughly chopped
½ bunch fresh parsley
  (about 25g / 1oz), roughly chopped
2 garlic cloves, roughly sliced
1 tsp ground cumin
½ tsp baking powder
1 tsp ground coriander
½ red chilli, finely chopped
2 spring onions, finely chopped
3 tbsp rapeseed oil

FOR THE SUMAC DRESSING

1 garlic clove, crushed
1 tsp sea salt
1 tsp sweet smoked paprika
4 tbsp extra virgin olive oil
2 tbsp lemon juice

FOR THE TOASTED QUINOA

30g (1¼ oz) quinoa
1 tbsp olive oil

TO ASSEMBLE

150g (5½oz) baby spinach, washed
1 avocado, peeled, stoned and sliced
1 beetroot, peeled and cut into
  fine matchsticks
seeds from 1 small pomegranate

Make the hummus. Put the chickpeas in the bowl of a food processor with 1½ tablespoons water and blitz until smooth. Add the rest of the ingredients and blitz for 2–3 minutes until smooth. Season to taste, transfer to a bowl, cover, and refrigerate.

Put all the falafel ingredients, except the oil, in the bowl of the food processor. Season to taste and pulse until you have a fairly smooth mixture – some chunks are fine. Using clean, wet hands, divide the mixture into four. Shape each piece into a round patty about 1.5cm (½in) thick.

Add the rapeseed oil to a heavy-based frying pan over a medium heat. When hot, add the falafel and fry for about 4–5 minutes on each side, or until golden and crisp. Remove the falafel from the pan and keep warm in the oven while you prepare the salad.

Put all the ingredients for the sumac dressing in a bowl and whisk well until combined. Set to one side until needed.

For the toasted quinoa, rinse two or three times in fresh cold water, then put it in a pan of salted water. Bring to a rolling boil, then reduce the heat and simmer for 8 minutes, or until the quinoa has puffed and doubled in size. Transfer to a strainer to drain off any excess water.

Heat the olive oil in the heavy-based frying pan over a medium heat and add the cooked quinoa. Using a wooden spoon, start moving the quinoa around the pan; as it gets hot and the excess water evaporates, it will start to pop and turn brown, and release a delicious nutty aroma. Once you get to this stage, remove the quinoa from the heat, transfer to a bowl, and allow to cool.

In a bowl, toss the spinach, avocado and beetroot with the sumanc dressing.

Spread 2 tablespoons of the hummus in the bottom of each of two serving bowls. Divide the salad between them. Top with the quinoa and falafel, sprinkle with pomegranate seeds and serve.

Kale, Asparagus and Beetroot Salad Bowl with Crispy Poached Eggs

//

SERVES / 2

TIME TAKEN / 50 minutes

6 asparagus spears
200g (7oz) kale leaves, stems removed
 and discarded
20g (¾oz) pine nuts
20g (¾oz) blanched whole almonds
20g (¾oz) blanched hazelnuts
20g (¾oz) pumpkin seeds
20g (¾oz) sunflower seeds
20g (¾oz) sesame seeds
2 tbsp runny honey
1 tsp sea salt
1 ripe avocado, sliced, to serve
2 prepped but not fried Crispy
 Poached Eggs (see page 16), to serve

FOR THE CHILLI FETA DRESSING

150g (5½oz) feta cheese
100g (3½oz) full fat yoghurt
zest and juice of 1 lemon
1 garlic clove, finely chopped
2 tbsp chopped dill
a pinch of dried chilli flakes

FOR THE PICKLED BEETROOT

4 tbsp olive oil
4 tbsp sherry vinegar
100ml (3½fl oz) maple syrup
1 garlic clove, finely chopped
1 large beetroot, peeled and chopped
 into matchsticks
sea salt and black pepper

Fill a large bowl with water and ice cubes and set aside.

Bring a large pan of water to the boil, then blanch the asparagus for 1–2 minutes, or until tender. Add the kale leaves to the pan and blanch for a further 30 seconds. Remove with a slotted spoon and plunge into the iced water – this stops them from overcooking and preserve the green colour. Drain and pat dry with a clean tea towel. Keep in the fridge until ready to assemble.

To make the pickled beetroot, put the oil, vinegar, maple syrup and garlic, in a small pan and bring to the boil. Remove from the heat and pour over the beetroot. Season and set aside to cool.

For the chilli feta dressing, put the feta in a bowl and roughly crumble with a fork. Add the rest of the dressing ingredients, season and mix well until combined. There should still be some lumps of feta visible, and the dressing consistency should be thick enough to coat the salad leaves – if it's too thick, add a drizzle of water. Refrigerate until you are about to assemble the salad.

Preheat the oven to 150°C fan/170°C/325°F/gas 3 and line a baking tray with parchment. In a small bowl, mix all the nuts and seeds with the honey and salt. Scatter the mixture onto the prepared tray and bake, stirring occasionally, for about 15–17 minutes or until golden brown. Remove from the oven and leave to cool slightly before roughly crushing the hazelnuts and almonds with the end of a rolling pin. Leave to cool completely.

Fry the crispy poached eggs as per the recipe on page 16.

To assemble the salad, gently toss together the kale, asparagus, and chilli feta dressing in a large bowl until the vegetables are well coated. Divide the salad greens into two serving bowls. Divide the pickled beetroot between the bowls and add the sliced avocado and crispy poached egg on top. Finish off with a generous sprinkling of the roasted nuts and seeds and serve.

Our Granola

//

MAKES / 600g (1lb 5oz)

TIME TAKEN / 1¼ hours

270g (9¾oz) jumbo porridge oats
25g (1oz) peeled pistachios
70g (2¾oz) whole almonds skin on
60g (2½oz) pumpkin seeds
65g (2½oz) sunflower seeds
70g (2¾oz) golden linseeds
120ml (4fl oz) olive oil
160ml (5½fl oz) maple syrup
60ml (2½fl oz) runny honey (use agave to make it vegan)
1 tsp vanilla extract
½ tsp ground cinnamon
½ tsp sea salt
35g (1½oz) coconut flakes

Preheat the oven to 160°C fan/180°C/350°F/ gas 4.

Combine the oats, pistachios, almonds and seeds in a mixing bowl.

Put the olive oil, maple syrup, honey, vanilla, cinnamon and salt in a small pan and gently bring to the boil. Pour onto the dry ingredients and stir well using a plastic spatula. Fully incorporate the syrup with the dry ingredients.

Tip the granola mix into a large, deep non-stick baking tray and spread evenly across the tray. Bake for 40–50 minutes, stirring every 15 minutes or so, to ensure the texture and crunch of the granola is even. During the last 10 minutes of cooking, add the coconut flakes and mix well. The coconut can burn so don't be tempted to add too soon.

Once the granola is golden and has a crunchy texture, remove from oven and allow to cool. While the granola is cooling, give it a mix every so often to prevent it from sticking to the tray.

Once cool, store in a large glass jar in a cool area. It will keep for up to 3 months.

Sunday Granola Bowl
with Yoghurt and Fruit

//

This granola bowl is our go-to healthy breakfast and is also super filling. Pears,
bananas and other hard fruits can be used if berries and stone fruits are not
available during winter months. Granola's a winner all year round!

SERVES / 2

TIME TAKEN / 5 minutes

8 heaped tbsp thick Greek yoghurt
8 tbsp Our Granola (see page 97)
2 apricots, peaches, nectarines or plums
  (whichever stone fruit you prefer)
6 raspberries
4 strawberries, sliced
8 blueberries
6 blackberries
2 tbsp runny honey
2 tsp bee pollen (optional)

Put 4 tablespoons Greek yoghurt into the bottom of
2 serving bowls. Sprinkle 4 tablespoons granola over
each bowl of yoghurt.

Now assemble the fruit evenly across both granola
bowls, arranging it as you wish. Drizzle with the honey,
then sprinkle the bee pollen across the fruit, if using,
and serve.

Quinoa Granola Bowl

//

This is a great alternative to our classic granola bowl if you're vegan. It really
sets you up for the day ahead. Coconut yoghurt is also a great alternative if
you're dairy-free or vegan.

SERVES / 2

TIME TAKEN / 5 minutes

8 tbsp cooked quinoa
500ml (17fl oz) almond milk
2 tbsp maple syrup
8 tbsp Our Granola (see page 97)
fruit, as above

Put 4 tablespoons quinoa into the bottom of 2 serving
bowls. Add half the almond milk to each bowl and
drizzle 1 tablespoon of maple syrup over each.

Top with the granola and fruit and serve.

Coconut, Red Lentil and Black-eyed Bean Curry

SERVES / 2

TIME TAKEN / 1 hour

1½ tbsp coconut oil
½ red onion, finely diced
1 tomato, finely diced
1 fresh lime leaf, crushed (to release
 the flavour)
200ml (7fl oz) coconut milk
100g (3½oz) dried red lentils,
 rinsed until the water runs clear
100g (3½oz) tinned black-eyed beans
 (drained weight)
40g (1½oz) baby spinach
1½ tbsp fish sauce
juice of 1 lime
1 tbsp sesame oil
1 tbsp soft dark brown sugar
sea salt and black pepper

FOR THE CURRY PASTE

1 garlic clove
2.5cm (1in) piece of fresh ginger,
 peeled and grated
½ serrano chilli, deseeded
½ stick lemongrass
½ bunch coriander (including stalks),
 roughly chopped
½ tsp ground cumin
½ tsp ground coriander
½ tsp ground turmeric
2 tbsp coconut oil

FOR THE COCONUT RELISH

1 tsp desiccated coconut
2 tbsp crème fraîche
5 sprigs of fresh coriander, shredded
2 leaves of fresh mint, shredded
½ tsp grated lime zest

TO SERVE

Scrambled Eggs (see page 19)
black sesame seeds
a few sprigs of fresh coriander
Crispy Spring Onion Pancakes
 (see page 101)

///

This warming, aromatic curry balances salt and sweet, sour and spicy flavours. It's great to make ahead and any leftovers can be kept in the fridge for up to a week. Use the coriander stems when making the paste as this will give it extra depth of flavour.

First, make the curry paste. Place all the ingredients in a bowl and purée with a hand blender (or use a food processor) until smooth. Add some water to loosen if you find it a bit stiff. Set aside.

Heat the coconut oil in a heavy-based pan over a medium–high heat. Add the onion and sauté for around 5 minutes until soft. Add the curry paste and cook for about 3 minutes until fragrant.

Add the diced tomato and lime leaf to the pan and stir, scraping up any brown bits that might have formed on the bottom. Cook for about 5 minutes until the tomato has softened, then pour in the coconut milk and 125ml (4fl oz) water and bring to a boil over a high heat.

Stir in the red lentils, then turn the heat down to medium. Cook for approximately 20 minutes until the lentils have softened and the curry has thickened, stirring occasionally to prevent sticking.

Add the black-eyed beans, spinach, fish sauce, lime juice, sesame oil and brown sugar to the pan, and stir until the spinach has wilted. Remove from the heat and season with salt and pepper.

Mix the ingredients for the coconut relish together in a small bowl and season with a pinch of salt. Refrigerate until needed.

Divide the curry between two bowls and top each with scrambled eggs and a generous tablespoon of coconut relish. Garnish with a sprinkling of black sesame seeds and some fresh coriander. Serve with the spring onion pancakes.

Crispy Spring Onion Pancakes

//

MAKES / 2

TIME TAKEN / 40 minutes

120g (3¾ oz) plain flour, plus extra for rolling
½ tsp salt
60ml (2½ fl oz) warm water
3 spring onions, finley sliced
3 tbsp rapeseed oil, for brushing
butter

Mix the flour and salt together in a mixing bowl. Make a well in the centre and pour in the warm water and 1 tablespoon of rapeseed oil. Mix using your hands until a dough just forms. Rest for 5 minutes.

On a lightly floured work surface, kneed the dough for 2–3 minutes until smooth. The dough should be soft when its ready. Rest for a further 20 minutes.

Divide the dough in half and roll each piece into a large circle on a floured work surface.

Brush the pancakes with rapeseed oil using a pastry brush and sprinkle the sliced spring onions evenly across both circles leaving 1cm (½in) around the edge clean.

Roll up the circle into a cylinder, crimping both ends of the pancake as you roll so that the spring onion doesn't fall out.

Next roll into the shape of a cinnamon roll or a snail, so that you have what looks like a circular spiral.

Roll the spiral into a flat circle. You will notice the spring onions all through the layers of the pancake which are created when you roll the dough into a cylinder.

For a simpler method, just add the spring onions to the dough and roll into a circle however, this will not produce the same texture and crispy layers.

Heat a medium non-stick frying pan and lightly brush with rapeseed oil, add 1 pancake and cook for 3–4 minutes on each side until golden and lightly crisp.

Rub each side of the pancake with a small piece of butter, repeat the process to make the other pancake then serve.

Salmon Kedgeree
with Beetroot Slaw

SERVES / 4

TIME TAKEN / 1½ hours

//

2 x 200g salmon fillets, skins removed
2 tbsp olive oil, plus extra for
    brushing and if needed
finely grated zest of 1 lemon
300g (10½oz) basmati rice
1 small onion, finely chopped
4 garlic cloves, finely chopped
2 tbsp ground coriander
2 tbsp ground cumin
1½ tbsp ground turmeric
6 cloves
6 black peppercorns
1 cinnamon stick
6 curry leaves
6 green cardamom pods, lightly
    crushed
1 tbsp sea salt
100g (3½oz) peas, steamed or boiled
sea salt and black pepper

FOR THE BEETROOT SLAW

2 medium raw beetroot, grated
1 garlic clove
4 tbsp white wine vinegar
2 tbsp olive oil
1 tbsp lemon juice
1 handful of fresh coriander, finely
    chopped
1 handful fresh mint, finely chopped

FOR THE CRISPY ONIONS

1 large onion, finely sliced
500ml (17fl oz) rapeseed oil

TO SERVE

4 Poached Eggs
1 handful of fresh parsley, chopped

This dish is designed to be shared. Served on a large platter, the different layers and textures will be a feast for the eyes and the palate. The fresh and vibrant beetroot slaw is a perfect accompaniment to the fragrant, spicy rice and the hearty salmon.

Combine all the ingredients for the beetroot slaw in a bowl and mix well. Cover and leave to rest in the fridge until needed.

Preheat the oven to 180°C fan/200°C/400°F/gas 6. Place the salmon fillets on a baking tray lined with parchment. Brush with olive oil, sprinkle with the lemon zest and season with salt and pepper. Bake for 15 minutes, or until just cooked, then allow to cool. Once cool, break into large flakes with a fork, and set aside.

Place the basmati rice in a large bowl and rinse under water until the water runs clear. Cover the rice with fresh water and leave to soak for 30 minutes. This will help to reduce the cooking time.

Heat the 2 tablespoons of oil in a large heavy-bottomed pan over a medium heat. Add the onion and sauté for about 5 minutes until it is translucent. Add the garlic and cook for 2 minutes. Add the coriander, cumin, turmeric, cloves, peppercorns, cinnamon, curry leaves and cardamom, and fry or a couple of minutes. Add some more oil if it becomes too dry – you want a paste-like consistency.

Drain the rice and add to the pan, mixing well to ensure that it is well coated with the spice paste. Add 600ml (21fl oz) water and salt. Increase the heat to high to bring it to the boil. Reduce the heat to low, cover, and simmer for around 30 minutes or until the rice is cooked.

While the rice is cooking, prepare the crispy onions. Heat the vegetable oil in a wok over a medium heat. Test the oil's heat by dropping in a slice of onion to test; if it dances and fizzes on the surface of the oil, the temperature is correct. Add the onions and fry until golden, stirring to make sure the onions nearest the wok edges don't burn. Using a slotted metal spoon, remove the onions from the oil when they are a shade or two lighter than your desired shade, as they will continue to cook after being removed from the oil. Place on kitchen paper to soak up any excess oil.

Just before the rice is cooked, remove the cinnamon stick, cloves and cardamom pods from the pan. Add the peas and cook for a couple of minutes as the rice finishes cooking.

Prepare the poached eggs as per the recipe on page 14.

To serve, spoon the rice onto a large platter. Top with the flaked salmon, poached eggs, crispy onions, and a generous amount of chopped parsley. Serve with the beetroot slaw on the side.

Steak with Sweet Potato Hash, Fried Eggs and Chimichurri

//

2 x 200g (7oz) sirloin steaks
2 garlic cloves, finely sliced
2 sprigs of rosemary
zest of 1 lemon
1 tbsp olive oil
2 tbsp rapeseed oil
4 eggs

FOR THE CHIMICHURRI

1 large shallot, finely diced
1 large red chilli, deseeded and
    finely diced
4 garlic cloves, finely chopped
100ml (3½fl oz) sherry vinegar
1 tsp flaked sea salt
½ tsp black pepper
25g (1oz) fresh coriander, finely
    chopped
25g (1oz) flat parsley, finely chopped
2 tbsp fresh oregano leaves
250ml (9fl oz) extra virgin olive oil

FOR THE SWEET POTATO HASH

500g (1lb 2oz) orange-fleshed sweet
    potato, peeled and diced
500g (1lb 2oz) white-fleshed sweet
    potato (Japanese), peeled and diced
500g (1lb 2oz) Maris Piper potatoes,
    peeled and diced into 1cm (½in)
    cubes
50ml (2fl oz) olive oil, plus extra for
    drizzling
1 large red onion, finely diced
3 garlic cloves, finely diced
80g (3oz) steamed or boiled peas
2 large handfuls of baby spinach
5 spring onions, finely diced
sea salt and black pepper

SERVES / 4

TIME TAKEN / 1¼ hours, plus marinating time

*This recipe is a real crowd pleaser and perfect for a large group
as steps 1–4 can be made in advance. The steak is best marinated
overnight and if you make the Chimichurri a few hours early it allows
the flavours to really mingle.*

First, make the chimichurri. Mix all the ingredients together in a
bowl. Cover and refrigerate for a few hours or overnight to allow
the flavours to mingle and deepen.

Next, prepare the steaks; in a dish large enough to accommodate
them in a single layer, mix together the garlic, rosemary, lemon
zest and olive oil. Add the steaks to the dish and rub the marinade
over them, massaging it in to ensure they're all well covered.
Cover and refrigerate for at least 2 hours, or ideally overnight.

For the hash, bring a large pan of salted water to the boil. Add
all the diced potatoes and bring back to the boil. Cook until just
tender – this should take about 5–7 minutes. You can test if they're
ready by taking a piece of potato and squashing it between your
fingers – if it yields, it's ready. Transfer to a colander and drain.

Place the potatoes in a single layer on a baking tray lined with
parchment. While they are still warm, drizzle with olive oil,
sprinkle with salt and pepper and mix with your hands so they are
well coated.

Heat 2 tablespoons oil in a large heavy-based frying pan over a
medium heat, and sauté the red onion and garlic gently for around
5–6 minutes until soft and golden brown. Remove from the heat.

Meanwhile, preheat the oven to it's lowest setting. Remove the
chimichurri and the steaks from the fridge. Discard the garlic and
rosemary from the marinade and allow the steaks to come to room
temperature while you continue with the potato hash.

Heat 2 tablespoons of oil in a large heavy-based frying pan on a medium heat. Put the potato cubes in the pan and cook for 15–20 minutes, turning frequently and pressing down with a spatula, until crispy and golden.

Add the onion and garlic mixture to the pan, along with the peas, spinach and spring onions. Toss through with the potatoes for a couple of minutes until the spinach has wilted, then season. Remove from the heat and transfer to a large heatproof dish. Place in the preheated oven to keep warm.

Wipe down the frying pan and return it to a medium–high heat. Season the steaks and place them in the pan. Cook for 2 minutes on each side for medium-rare, or longer to your liking. Remove from the pan, along with any juices, and cover with foil to rest.

Wipe down the frying pans and return to a medium–high heat. Add the rapeseed oil and let it heat up, then fry the eggs to your liking.

Slice the steaks. Transfer the sweet potato hash to a large serving platter and top with the steak and fried eggs. Drizzle generously with the chimichurri and any reserved juices from the steak before serving.

Baking the Sunday Way

Our Banana Bread

//

SERVES / 6–8

TIME TAKEN / 1½ hours

75g (2½oz) unsalted butter
4 over-ripe bananas
200g (7oz) dark brown soft sugar
1 large egg, lightly beaten
190g (6¾oz) plain flour, sifted
1 tsp vanilla extract
5 medjool dates, pitted and roughly chopped
1 tsp bicarbonate of soda
a pinch of sea salt
1 tsp ground cinnamon
½ tsp freshly grated nutmeg

FOR THE CINNAMON BUTTER
25g (1oz) salted butter
a pinch of ground cinnamon

Preheat the oven to 160°C fan/180°C/350°F/ gas 4, and line a large non-stick loaf pan with parchment.

Gently melt the butter in a pan over a low heat, then set aside to cool slightly.

Put the bananas in a large mixing bowl and crush with a fork until broken down but not smooth.

Add the sugar and egg to the mashed banana and mix until incorporated. Then add the flour, vanilla, dates, bicarbonate of soda, salt, cinnamon, nutmeg and melted butter. Using a spatula, fold everything together for 3 minutes, to ensure that there are no flour lumps in the mix. The batter will not be smooth as there will be small pieces of banana and dates visible, which will give the bread a yummy texture once cooked.

Transfer the batter to the prepared loaf tin and bake for 45–50 minutes until risen and golden and a skewer inserted into the centre comes out clean. Remove from the oven and allow to cool for 20 minutes before transferring to a wire rack to cool completely.

For the cinnamon butter, mix the butter with the cinnamon until it's well incorporated.

Slice the bread and serve toasted with cinnamon butter.

Cornbread with Chipotle and Maple Butter

//

MAKES / 1 large loaf (or 20–24 small muffins)
TIME TAKEN / 1 hr 20 minutes

185g (6½oz) unsalted butter, melted
3 eggs, lightly beaten
375ml (13fl oz) whole milk
1 tbsp honey
1 tbsp caster sugar
375g (13oz) plain flour, sifted
225g (8oz) fine cornmeal
1½ tsp baking powder
½ bunch coriander, finely chopped
½ red chilli, halved, deseeded and finely diced
4 spring onions, finely sliced
1 tsp sea salt

FOR THE CHIPOTLE AND MAPLE BUTTER
200g (7oz) unsalted butter
1 tbsp maple syrup
2 tsp coriander, chopped
½ chipotle chilli, finely chopped
sea salt and black pepper

Preheat the oven to 160°C fan/170°C/325°F/gas 3. Grease and line a 900g (2lb) loaf tin neatly with parchment, or fill a couple of 12-hole muffin tins with paper cases.

First, make the chipotle and maple butter. Using an electric whisk, whip the butter for 1 minute until pale and fluffy, then fold in the maple syrup, coriander and chipotle chilli. Season with salt and pepper. Cut a large piece of parchment and place the chipotle butter inside, roll into a cylinder, folding in both ends of the parchment and refrigerate.

For the cornbread, gently melt the butter in a small pan, then set aside and allow to cool.

In a mixing bowl, whisk together the eggs, milk, honey and sugar. Add the flour and cornmeal along with the baking powder

and mix again. Now add the cooled melted butter, coriander, chilli, spring onions and salt, and mix until everything is combined.

Pour the cornbread mix into the prepared loaf tin. If you are using muffin cases, fill those three-quarters full.

Bake until risen and golden – around 50–60 minutes for the loaf, or 20–30 minutes for the muffins. Insert a skewer into the centre – if it comes out clean, the cornbread is ready.

Remove from oven and allow to cool in the tin for 20 minutes before turning out onto a wire rack to cool completely. The cornbread will keep for up to 5 days in the fridge.

Serve toasted with a slice of chipotle and maple butter.

Gluten-free Carrot Cake

///

SERVES / 12

PREP TIME / 1 hour, plus cooling

125ml (4fl oz) rapeseed oil, plus extra for greasing
440g (15½oz) ground almonds
75g (2½oz) flaked almonds
70g (2¾oz) large plump sultanas
70g (2¾oz) coconut flakes
375g (13oz) carrots, peeled and grated
1 tsp baking powder
½ tsp freshly grated nutmeg
1 tsp ground ginger
1 tsp ground cinnamon
5 large eggs
250g (9oz) soft light brown sugar
1 tsp vanilla extract

FOR THE CREAM CHEESE FROSTING
150g (5½oz) cream cheese
1 tbsp caster sugar
1 tsp vanilla extract

TO SERVE
4 tbsp Our Granola (see page 97)
fresh berries

Preheat the oven to 160°C fan/180°C/350°F/ gas 4. Grease a non-stick 25cm (10in) round springform cake tin and line the base with parchment.

Put the ground almonds, flaked almonds, sultanas, coconut flakes, grated carrots, baking powder, nutmeg, ginger and cinnamon into a large mixing bowl. Stir and set aside.

Put the eggs and the sugar in a bowl of an electric mixer fitted with a whisk attachment. Whisk on a high speed for 8 minutes, or until the mix has doubled in volume and thickened. Add the vanilla.

Reduce the mixer to medium speed. Slowly pour the oil into the bowl, being careful not to add it too quickly. Continue to mix for a further 3 minutes.

Fold the egg mixture into the dry ingredients using a plastic spatula, making sure all the ingredients are fully incorporated.

Transfer the mixture to the prepared tin and bake for 40–45 minutes, or until a skewer inserted into the centre comes out clean. Remove from the oven and leave to cool in the tin.

To make the frosting, mix together the cream cheese, sugar and vanilla in a bowl until smooth.

Once the cake is completely cool, remove from the tin and place on serving dish. Gently spread the frosting evenly across the top of the cake, then add a generous sprinkle of granola on top. Serve with fresh berries.

Feta and Olive Cake

//

MAKES / 1 loaf
TIME TAKEN / 1½ hours

225ml (7¾fl oz) sunflower oil, plus extra for greasing
3 eggs
250ml (9fl oz) milk
3 spring onions, finely sliced
100g (3½oz) Kalamata olives, pitted and chopped
200g (7oz) feta cheese, diced into 2cm cubes
65g (2¼oz) Sunblush tomatoes, finely sliced
4 tbsp chopped coriander
4 tbsp chopped mint
320g (11¼oz) self-raising flour
1 tsp baking powder
1 heaped tsp sunflower seeds
1 heaped tsp black sesame seeds
1 heaped tsp white sesame seeds
butter, for spreading, to serve

Preheat the oven to 160°C fan/180°C/350°F/ gas 4. Grease a large loaf tin with oil, then line the base with parchment.

Whisk the eggs in a large bowl, then stir in the milk and oil. Add the spring onions, olives, feta cheese, Sunblush tomatoes, coriander and mint, and stir again. Sift in the flour and baking powder and mix until combined.

Pour the mixture into the prepared loaf tin and sprinkle the sunflower seeds and black and white sesame seeds over the top. Bake for 50–60 minutes, or until a skewer inserted into the centre comes out clean. Remove from the oven and allow to cool for 20 minutes before removing from the tin and placing on a cooling rack to cool completely.

Cut the cake into generous slices and serve toasted and buttered.

Gluten-free Lemon Polenta Cake

//

SERVES / 12

PREP TIME / 1¼ hours

335g (11¾oz) unsalted butter, softened,
plus extra for greasing
335g (11¾oz) caster sugar
4 large eggs
335g (11¾oz) ground almonds
165g (5¾oz) polenta
1 tsp vanilla extract
zest and juice of 3 lemons

FOR THE GROUP PLATTER

4 tbsp thick Greek yoghurt
4 tsp Berry Compote (see page 149)
4 tbsp Apple Compote (see page 149)
150g (6oz) blackberries
150g (6oz) raspberries
115g (4oz) strawberries, washed and halved
1 large handful of blueberries
2 passion fruit, halved
1 handful of fresh mint sprigs
3 tbsp Our Granola (see page 97)
icing sugar, for dusting

Preheat the oven to 160°C fan/180°C/350°F/gas 4. Grease a non-stick 25cm (10in) round springform cake tin and line the base with parchment.

Put the butter and sugar into the bowl of an electric mixer fitted with a paddle attachment and mix on a medium speed for 5–8 minutes until it becomes pale and creamy.

Add the eggs one at a time, making sure each egg is well incorporated before adding the next one. You will need to scrape down the side of the bowl using a plastic spatula during this process.

Once all the eggs have been added, lower the speed to a slow pace and add the ground almonds and polenta 1 tablespoon at a time, then mix for a further 2 minutes.

Add the vanilla extract along with the lemon zest and juice, then return to a medium speed and continue to mix for a further 3 minutes to ensure all the ingredients are fully incorporated. The mixture should be smooth and have a fluffy consistency.

Transfer the mixture to the cake tin and bake for 45–50 minutes until golden brown and a skewer inserted into the centre comes out clean. Remove from the oven and leave to cool in the tin.

To make the group platter, preheat the oven to 130°C fan/150°C/300°F/gas 2 and line a baking tray with parchment.

Place 4 slices of cake onto the prepared baking tray and warm in the oven for 10 minutes. Remove the cake from the oven and gently cut each slice in half.

Arrange the cake pieces onto a large serving platter, add the yoghurt, berry and apple compotes. Scatter the berries over the platter, and spoon over the seeds from one of the the passion fruit, adding the other fruit halves. Add a few mint sprigs, sprinkle with the granola, dust with icing sugar and serve.

Toasted Coconut Bread
with Plum Compote and Almond Brittle

//

SERVES / 6

PREP TIME / 1 hour 20 minutes

115g (4oz) unsalted butter, softened,
plus extra for greasing
190g (6¾oz) plain flour, sifted
150g (5oz) desiccated coconut
¼ tsp sea salt
1½ tsp baking powder
160g (5¾oz) caster sugar, plus 1 tsp
3 large eggs
120ml (4fl oz) double cream
120ml (4fl oz) coconut milk
zest of 1 orange
1 tsp vanilla extract

FOR THE CREAM CHEESE

3 tbsp cream cheese
½ tsp vanilla extract
1 tsp caster sugar

FOR THE PLUM COMPOTE

4 plums
juice of ½ orange
1 tbsp caster sugar

TO SERVE

150g (5oz) blackberries
Almond Brittle (see page 69)
4 fresh mint leaves, finely chopped
icing sugar, for dusting

Preheat the oven to 160°C fan/180°C/350°F/gas 4. Grease and line a large non-stick loaf tin with parchment, taking care to make it neat along the edges so that you get a clean finish when the cake is cooked.

In a large bowl, combine the flour, coconut, salt and baking powder and set aside.

Put the butter and sugar into the bowl of a stand mixer fitted with a paddle attachment and beat on a medium speed for 6–8 minutes until pale and fluffy.

Add the eggs one at a time, making sure each egg is thoroughly incorporated before adding the next. Reduce to a slow speed then add the flour mix. Once incorporated, add the cream, coconut milk, orange zest and vanilla extract. Continue to mix for a further 3 minutes.

Pour the cake batter into the prepared tin and bake for 40–45 minutes, or until a skewer inserted into the centre comes out clean. Remove from the oven and leave to cool in the tin.

In a small bowl, mix the cream cheese with the vanilla and caster sugar. Refrigerate until needed.

To make the plum compote, put the plums in a small pan with the orange juice and sugar. Cook over a medium heat for 6–8 minutes until the plums have slightly broken down and a syrup has formed.

To assemble, slice 2 pieces coconut bread per person and toast until golden on both sides. Lay on the plate, add the cream cheese, plum compote and a few blackberries. Sprinkle over the almond brittle and mint. Dust with icing sugar.

Tahini and Honey Flatbreads

//

These flatbreads are extremely versatile and the perfect partner to merguez sausages
and poached eggs (see page 32). Use kitchen paper to wipe out the pan after each
flatbread has been cooked as the tahini and honey mix will ooze out whilst they cook.

MAKES / 4

TIME TAKEN / 40 minutes

2 tbsp tahini
1 tbsp honey
150g (5½oz) self-raising flour, plus extra if needed
½ tsp sea salt
½ tsp baking powder
150g (5½oz) full fat Greek yoghurt
olive oil, for brushing
za'atar, to garnish

Put the tahini and honey in a small bowl and mix using a fork until combined. Set aside until needed.

Combine the flour, salt and baking powder in a large bowl, add the yoghurt and mix with a spatula until a dough starts to form. Transferto a clean work surface and continue to bring together with your hands until you have a smooth, soft dough – it shouldn't be sticky, so add a touch more flour if needed.

Divide the dough into four even pieces. Dust the surface with flour and, using a rolling pin, roll each flat bread into circle roughly 8cm (3¼in) in diameter. They don't need to be perfect, so don't stress!

Spread a quarter of the tahini and honey mixture evenly across the top of each flatbread. Fold each flatbread in half and then in half again, so that they form triangle shapes. This step is necessary so that when you roll out the breads the tahini and honey will be spread throughout. Lightly dust the surface with flour and roll the flatbreads out again to rough 8cm (3¼in) circles.

Heat a non-stick frying pan over a medium heat. Once hot, add a flatbread and cook for 3–4 minutes on each side. Bubbles will start to form on the top of the bread when cooking; this is a good indicator of when to turn over. The flatbread should be lightly coloured on both sides when ready.

Remove from the pan and lightly brush with olive oil. Repeat to cook the remaining three flatbreads, wiping the pan clean between each one with kitchen paper, if necessary. Sprinkle with za'atar and serve immediately or warm in the oven when needed, but use the same day.

Crumpets

//

You will need three crumpet rings for this recipe. The crumpets can be kept in the fridge for 2 days, they'll just need to be toasted. Use a cloth to remove the rings from the crumpets as the metal handles will become hot.

MAKES / 8

TIME TAKEN / 30 minutes, plus proving time

275ml (10fl oz) whole milk
225g (8oz) strong white bread flour
7g (¼oz) dried yeast
½ tsp caster sugar
½ tsp sea salt
1 tbsp butter, melted, for greasing, plus extra butter, to serve
jam, to serve (optional)

Put the milk in a small pan with 3½ tablespoons water and heat over a low heat for a few minutes until just hot. Remove from the heat and set aside.

Combine the flour, yeast, sugar and salt in a mixing bowl. Make a well in the centre, and pour in the milk, stirring with a metal spoon until you have a smooth thick batter; it's important not to overmix or the crumpets may be tough. Cover with a clean cloth and place in a warm place for 50 minutes to prove. The batter will start to rise and become sticky.

Place a large non-stick frying pan over a low heat and brush the base with a little melted butter. Brush the inside of 3 crumpet rings with butter, too, and place in the pan.

Stir the batter, then spoon 3 tablespoons into each ring. Cook for 10–12 minutes until the tops of the crumpets are just cooked – bubbles should appear and pop on the surface. Remove the rings (with a cloth, as they will be hot), turn the crumpets over, and cook for 1 minute more. Remove the crumpets from the pan using a spatula and repeat to cook the remaining crumpets.

Serve toasted with lots of butter and jam, if you like.

Jams
the
Sunday
Way

Making Jam

//

We prefer to make our own preserves as shop-bought Jam is never as good as when you make it yourself. We generally try to use the fruit that's in season. Our veg man gives us a call to let us know what's available and then we talk about the flavours that might work together, trying to be a bit interesting and original. We also selfishly imagine the flavours that we'd want to eat at home!

Here are a few tips that will be useful for preparing the recipes on the following pages.

STERILISING YOUR JARS

If you want your jam to keep for months or even years, you will need to make sure you prepare the jars properly.

First, wash the jars using hot soapy water, then put upside down in dishwasher and run a hot wash without detergent. The jars will need to be warm when filled so it's all about timing. If no dishwasher is available, you can also place jars in a large pot of water and slowly increase the temperature until the water boils. Once the is boiling, leave the jars in the pan for a maximum of 10 minutes then remove from the pan and leave to drain until they are warm and ready to fill.

GETTING STARTED

The first stage of making the jam is very important: make sure you allow the fruit and sugar time to rest once mixed and before cooking. Don't be tempted to cook the jam before the sugar has softened the fruit as the sugar won't breakdown properly and is likely to burn and discolour the jam. We follow this process when making all our fruit jams.

CHECKING IF THE JAM IS READY

Before making the jam, put a small saucer in the freezer to chill as its important the saucer is cold when testing the jam. When you think the jam is ready, pour a teaspoon of it onto the chilled saucer. Push it with a finger – if it's ready it should wrinkle slightly and be thicker in texture. If it slides about like a liquid, then it hasn't reached setting point and should be cooked for longer.

Once you open a jar of jam, you will need to store it in the fridge.

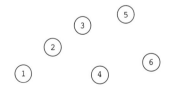

1   Peach and pomegranate
2   Strawberry and passion fruit
3   Apricot and fig
4   Summer berry and vanilla
5   Plum and lemon verbena
6   Rhubarb, strawberry and stem ginger

Rhubarb, Strawberry and Stem Ginger Jam

//

MAKES / 4 x 225g (8oz) jars

TIME TAKEN / 1 hour

300g (10½oz) fresh rhubarb (preferably as pink as possible), cut into 2.5cm (1in) pieces
500g (1lb 2oz) fresh strawberries, halved
6 pieces stem ginger, finely chopped
500g (1lb 2oz) jam sugar

Wash and sterilise your jars according to the instructions on page 128. They will need to be hot when you fill them.

Place a small saucer or two in the freezer to chill, to use for testing the jam is set.

Put the rhubarb, strawberries, stem ginger and sugar into a non-stick pan and mix together. Set aside for 20 minutes until the sugar has almost dissolved and the fruit has softened.

Put the pan over a low heat and simmer for 5 minutes until the rhubarb and strawberries are soft. You can gently crush the fruit using a fork or whisk while simmering, but don't break them up too much as its important to have texture in the jam.

Turn the heat up and bring to the boil, then continue to boil until a sugar thermometer has reached 105°C (221°F). The jam will usually take between 20–30 minutes to cook. Stir occasionally as it cooks so that it doesn't catch on the bottom of the pan. If you don't have a thermometer, you can also test if it is ready by following the steps on page 128. If it hasn't reached setting point, it should be returned to the heat and cooked for a few more minutes before testing again.

Once the jam is ready, carefully pour it into the warm, sterilised jars and screw the lids on to completely seal the jars. Keep ambient and refrigerate once opened.

Peach and Pomegranate Jam

//

MAKES / 3 x 225g (8oz) jars

TIME TAKEN / 1 hour

750g (1lb 10oz) fresh peaches, stones removed and quartered
500g (1lb 2oz) jam sugar
seeds of 1 pomegranate
juice of 1 lime

Wash and sterilise your jars according to the instructions on page 128. They will need to be hot when you fill them.

Place a small saucer or two in the freezer to chill, to use for testing the jam is set.

Put the peaches and sugar into a non-stick pan and stir together. Set aside for 20 minutes until the sugar has almost dissolved and the fruit has softened.

Put the pomegranate seeds into a food processor and blend for 2 minutes. Pour the pomegranate into a fine muslin-lined strainer and drain all the juice from blended seeds, using the muslin cloth squeeze out all the excess juice from the pomegranate seeds.

Add the pomegranate juice and lime juice to the peaches and sugar, and mix well. Put the

pan over a low heat and simmer for 5–8 minutes until the peaches have softened.

Turn the heat up and bring to the boil, then continue to boil until a sugar thermometer has reached 105°C (221°F). The jam will usually take between 20–30 minutes to cook. Stir occasionally as it cooks so that it doesn't catch on the bottom of the pan. If you don't have a thermometer, you can also test if it is ready by following the steps on page 128. If it hasn't reached setting point, it should be returned to the heat and cooked for a few more minutes before testing again.

Once the jam is ready, carefully pour it into the warm, sterilised jars and screw the lids on to completely seal the jars. Refrigerate once opened.

Summer Berry and Vanilla Jam

//

MAKES / 4 x 225g (8oz) jars

TIME TAKEN / 1 hour

800g (1lb 12oz) mixed fresh summer berries (use frozen if fresh berries are not available)
2 tsp vanilla extract or 1 vanilla pod
500g (1lb 2oz) jam sugar

Wash and sterilise your jars according to the instructions on page 128. They will need to be hot when you fill them.

Place a small saucer or two in the freezer to chill, to use for testing the jam is set.

Put the mixed berries, vanilla and sugar into a non-stick pan and mix together. Set aside for 20 minutes until the sugar has almost dissolved and the fruit has softened.

Put the pan over a low heat and simmer for 5 minutes until the berries have completely softened. You can gently crush the fruit using a fork or whisk while simmering, but don't break them up too much as its important to have texture in the jam.

Turn the heat up and bring to the boil, then continue to boil until a sugar thermometer has reached 105°C (221°F). The jam will usually take between 20–30 minutes to cook. Stir occasionally as it cooks so that it doesn't catch on the bottom of the pan. If you don't have a thermometer, you can also test if it is ready by following the steps on page 128. If it hasn't reached setting point, it should be returned to the heat and cooked for a few more minutes before testing again.

Once the jam is ready, carefully pour it into the warm, sterilised jars and screw the lids on to completely seal the jars. Refrigerate once opened.

Strawberry and Passion Fruit Jam

//

MAKES / 3 x 225g (8oz) jars

TIME TAKEN / 1 hour

750g (1lb 10oz) fresh strawberries, washed, stems removed and halved
pulp and seeds of 2 passion fruit
500g (1lb 2oz) jam sugar

Wash and sterilise your jars according to the instructions on page 128. They will need to be hot when you fill them.

Place a small saucer or two in the freezer to chill, to use for testing the jam is set.

Put the strawberries, passion fruit and sugar into a non-stick pan and mix together. Set aside for 20 minutes until the sugar has almost dissolved and the fruit has softened.

Put the pan over a low heat and simmer for 5 minutes until the strawberries are soft. You can gently crush the strawberries using a fork or whisk while it is simmering, but don't break them up too much as its important to have texture.

Turn the heat up and bring to the boil, then continue to boil until a sugar thermometer has reached 105°C (221°F). The jam will usually take between 20–30 minutes to cook. Stir occasionally as it cooks so that it doesn't catch on the bottom of the pan. If you don't have a thermometer, you can also test if it is ready by following the steps on page 128. If it hasn't reached setting point, it should be returned to the heat and cooked for a few more minutes before testing again.

Once the jam is ready, carefully pour it into the warm, sterilised jars and screw the lids on to completely seal the jars. Refrigerate once opened.

Plum and Lemon Verbena Jam

//

MAKES / 3 x 300g (11oz) jars

TIME TAKEN / 1 hour

800g (1lb 12oz) fresh ripe plums (Victoria variety
if available), halved and stones removed
500g (1lb 2oz) jam sugar
6 lemon verbena leaves, torn
juice of ½ lemon
½ tsp vanilla extract

Wash and sterilise your jars according to the instructions on page 128. They will need to be hot when you fill them.

Place a small saucer or two in the freezer to chill, to use for testing the jam is set.

Put the plums, sugar and verbena leaves into a non-stick pan and mix together. Set aside for 20 minutes until the sugar has almost dissolved and the plums have softened.

Add the lemon juice and vanilla to the pan and mix well. Put the pan over a low heat and simmer for 5–8 minutes until the plums have softened.

Turn the heat up and bring to the boil, then continue to boil until a sugar thermometer has reached 105°C (221°F). The jam will usually take between 20–30 minutes to cook. Stir occasionally as it cooks so that it doesn't catch on the bottom of the pan. If you don't have a thermometer, you can also test if it is ready by following the steps on page 128. If it hasn't reached setting point, it should be returned to the heat and cooked for a few more minutes before testing again.

Once the jam is ready, carefully pour it into the warm, sterilised jars and screw the lids on to completely seal the jars. Refrigerate once opened.

Apricot and Fig Jam

//

MAKES / 4 x 225ml (8oz) jars

TIME TAKEN / 1 hour

500g (1lb 2oz) fresh ripe apricots, halved and stoned
250g (9oz) fresh ripe figs, quartered
2 tsp vanilla extract or 1 vanilla pod
500g (1lb 2oz) jam sugar (sugar with added pectin)

Wash and sterilise your jars according to the instructions on page 128. They will need to be hot when you fill them.

Place a small saucer or two in the freezer to chill, to use for testing the jam is set.

Put the apricots, figs, vanilla and sugar into a non-stick pan and mix together. Set aside for 20 minutes until the sugar has almost dissolved and the fruit has softened.

Put the pan over a low heat and simmer for 5 minutes until the fruit has completely softened. You can gently crush the fruit using a fork or whisk while simmering, but don't break them up too much as its important to have texture in the jam.

Turn the heat up and bring to the boil, then continue to boil until a sugar thermometer has reached 105°C (221°F). The jam will usually take between 20–30 minutes to cook. Stir occasionally so that it doesn't catch on the bottom of the pan.If you don't have a thermometer, you can also test if it is ready by following the steps on page 128. If it hasn't reached setting point, it should be returned to the heat and cooked for a few more minutes before testing again.

Once the jam is ready, carefully pour it into the warm, sterilised jars and screw the lids on to completely seal the jars. Refrigerate once opened.

Chilli Jam

///

Chilli jam is a good way to use up overripe tomatoes. The aromatic flavours of the ginger, garlic and lime help balance the the chilli and it is great served with eggs.

MAKES / 1 x 400g (14oz) jar
TIME TAKEN / 1 hour

500g (1lb 2oz) ripe tomatoes
4 red chillies
5 garlic cloves, peeled
2 thumbs ginger (approx 25g / 1oz), peeled
2 tbsp fish sauce (optional)
300g (10½oz) caster sugar
100ml (3½oz) red wine vinegar
2 tbsp lime juice

Wash and sterilise your jars according to the instructions on page 128. They will need to be hot when you fill them.

Place a small saucer or two in the freezer to chill, to use for testing the jam is set.

Using a stick blender or food processor, purée together the tomatoes, chillies, garlic, ginger and fish sauce.

Put the puréed tomato mixture in a pan with the sugar and vinegar. Gently bring to the boil over a medium heat, then continue to boil until a sugar thermometer has reached 105°C (221°F), then turn down to low to simmer for 30 minutes, stirring from time to time so it doesn't catch and burn.

Once the jam has thickened and reduced to about a third, it's done.

If you don't have a thermometer, you can also test if it is ready by following the steps on page 128. If it hasn't reached setting point, it should be returned to the heat and cooked for a few more minutes before testing again.

Once ready, carefully pour the jam into the warm, sterilised jar and screw the lid on to completely seal. The jam can be kept for up to 6 months. Refrigerate once opened.

Bacon Jam

//

Sounds weird right? We thought so too at first, but this is a jam that combines salty and sweet flavours to give the most amazing outcome. It can be spread on toast or used in a variety of different types of sandwiches and is a great secret weapon to have in the fridge for when you crave something indulgent.

MAKES / 2 X 450g (1lb) jars

TIME TAKEN / 1 hour

700g (1lb 9oz) streaky bacon
2 red onions, sliced
1 Spanish onion, sliced
4 garlic cloves, minced

2 red chillies, finely diced
1 tsp smoked paprika
¼ tsp sea salt
¼ tsp black pepper
250ml (9fl oz) maple syrup
125ml (4fl oz) bourbon whiskey
75g (2½oz) soft dark brown sugar
4 tbsp red wine vinegar

Preheat the oven to 170°C fan/190°C/375°F/gas 5 and line a lipped baking tray with parchment.

Place the bacon in a single layer on the prepared baking tray. Cook in the oven for about 15 minutes, or until just starting to turn golden and crisp – you don't want it to get too crisp. Remove from the oven and transfer to kitchen paper to absorb the excess fat. (Plenty of flavoursome bacon fat will have accumulated in the baking tray, too – don't get rid of that yet as you'll need it shortly.) When cool enough to handle, roughly chop the bacon into small pieces.

Heat 6 tablespoons of the reserved bacon fat in a large heavy-based frying pan over a medium heat. Add the sliced red and Spanish onions and cook for around 8–10 minutes until caramelised. Add the garlic and cook for another 4 minutes. Add the chopped chilli, smoked paprika and salt and pepper, and stir to combine. Remove from the

heat and add the maple syrup and bourbon. Return to the heat and cook the mixture for 2–3 minutes, stirring continuously. Add the sugar and vinegar and cook for a further 2–3 minutes until the sugar has dissolved.

Add the chopped bacon, lower the heat, and simmer gently for a further 10 minutes until the mixture is thick and glossy. You're looking for a syrup-like consistency; if the jam is too thick, add some water to loosen it.

Remove the jam from the heat and allow it to cool slightly. Transfer to a food processor and pulse until everything is well combined but not completely smooth – it should still have some texture.

Pour the jam into sterilised jam jars, seal and keep in the fridge for up to 2 months. Serve at room temperature when needed.

Condiments
the
Sunday
Way

Harissa

//

1 red pepper
4 tbsp olive oil, plus 1 tsp for
   drizzling
1 tbsp cumin seeds
1 tsp coriander seeds
1 tsp carraway seeds
1 tsp smoked paprika
200g (7oz) red chillies, deseeded
1 garlic clove, peeled
2 tbsp red wine vinegar
sea salt and black pepper

Preheat the oven to 170°C fan/190°C/375°F/gas 5.

Place the whole red pepper on a small roasting tray, drizzle with 1 teaspoon of olive oil and season with a pinch of salt and pepper. Roast for 25 minutes, or until the skin has slightly blackened. Remove the pepper from the oven, put it in a bowl, cover with cling film, and set aside for 5 minutes. This will steam the pepper so that the skin is easily removed. Discard the skin and deseed the pepper.

Put the spice seeds in a small non-stick frying pan and gently toast over a medium heat for a few minutes until lightly coloured and they release their aroma. Add the paprika. Crush the toasted spices using a pestle and mortar until finely ground.

Put the chillies and garlic into a food processor and pulse in short bursts until you have a course texture. Add the roasted pepper, toasted spices, olive oil and vinegar to the food processor and continue to pulse for a further 30 seconds, or until all the ingredients are fully incorporated. Season with salt and pepper.

Transfer to a jar and store in the fridge. The harissa will keep for 7 days.

Dukkah

//

Dukkah is the perfect
accompaniment for our courgette
fritters, but it's also great sprinkled
on fried or scrambled eggs.
It rocks on salads too!

50g (1¾oz) whole blanched almonds
50g (1¾oz) whole blanched hazelnuts
50g (1¾oz) walnut halves
40g (1½oz) pumpkin seeds
2 tsp sesame seeds
2 tsp coriander seeds
20g (¾oz) cumin seeds
2 tsp sumac
1 tsp flaked sea salt
1 tsp black pepper

Preheat the oven to 160°C fan/180°C/350°C/gas 4 and line a large baking tray with parchment.

Put all the ingredients in a large mixing bowl and mix well with a wooden spoon.

Evenly spread the dukkah mix across the prepared tray. Bake for 30–35 minutes, mixing after 15 minutes to ensure even roasting. The spices will release an amazing aroma and the nuts should be gently roasted with a light golden colour when ready. Remove from the oven and set aside to cool.

Once cool, put the dukkah into a food processor and use the pulse button to gradually break up the mixture to a very coarse breadcrumb consistency. Don't put the machine on and leave it, as the nuts will be ground too fine and become a powder. A pestle and mortar can also be used, it just takes longer!

Store in an airtight jar and keep at room temperature for up to 6 months.

Labneh

MAKES / 500g (1lb 2oz)
TIME TAKEN / 10 minutes,
plus 12 hours straining time

*Labneh is a strained yoghurt
which is made by removing most
of the whey, resulting in a thicker,
creamier consistency while keeping
its distinctive sour taste. This is the
basic recipe, to which you can add
any number of herbs and spices. We
like it with crushed peppercorns.*

*1 tsp sea salt
zest of 1 lemon
500g (1lb 2oz) full-fat yoghurt*

Stir the salt and lemon zest into the yoghurt.

Line a strainer with a few layers of cheesecloth. Set the
strainer over a deep bowl with at least 7cm (2¾in) between
the bottom of the bowl and the strainer. Scrape the
yoghurt mix into the lined strainer and fold the ends of the
cheesecloth over the yoghurt so it is covered. Refrigerate for
12 hours and then it's ready. The whey (the liquid that has
collected in the bowl) can be discarded or used to make a
delicious raspberry soda (see page 166).

Store the labneh (in the cheesecloth) in a sealable container
in the fridge for up to a week.

Mint Yoghurt

MAKES / 4–6 portions
TIME TAKEN / 10 minutes

*100g (3½oz) full fat Greek yoghurt
60g (2oz) bunch of mint, picked and
 shredded
60g (2oz) coriander, finely chopped
1 garlic clove, finely chopped
zest and juice of 1 lemon
sea salt and black pepper*

Pour the yoghurt into a fine strainer and leave it to drain for
5 minutes. This will remove any excess liquid.

Put the yoghurt in a large bowl and add the mint, coriander
and chopped garlic. Mix well until all herbs are incorporated
into the yoghurt.

Add the lemon zest and juice and season with salt and
pepper. Mix well again and taste to check the seasoning.
Store in the fridge until ready to serve.

Tahini Lemon Yoghurt

MAKES / 150g (5½oz)
TIME TAKEN / 5 minutes

//

125g (4½oz) thick Greek yoghurt
25g (1oz) tahini
1 garlic clove, finely chopped
zest and juice of 1 large lemon
sea salt and black pepper

Put the yoghurt in a small mixing bowl. Add the tahini, garlic, and lemon zest and juice. Mix well and season with salt and pepper. Mix again and refrigerate until needed.

The tahini yoghurt will keep in the fridge for up to 5 days.

Beetroot and Dill Purée

MAKES / 6–8 portions
TIME TAKEN / 1½ hours

//

We serve this with the salt beef potato pancake dish (see page 85). It's also great with omelettes, in salads, and as a spread in sandwiches too.

4 medium beetroots, washed
2 garlic cloves, peeled
2 tbsp olive oil
1 tbsp apple cider vinegar
1 heaped tbsp thick Greek yoghurt
½ small bunch dill, finely chopped
sea salt and black pepper

Put the beetroot into a pan, add a pinch of salt and cover with water, making sure the beetroot are completely submerged. Bring the water to the boil and cook for 1–1¼ hours, or until the beetroot is cooked through. Use a small knife to pierce the beetroot – if the knife goes in easily it is ready. Drain and set aside to cool for 15 minutes. Once cool, remove the skin from the beetroot and cut into quarters.

Place the beetroot quarters into a food processor along with the garlic, olive oil and vinegar. Season with salt and pepper, and blend until you have a smooth purée.

Transfer the purée to a bowl and, using a spatula, fold in the Greek yoghurt and dill until fully incorporated. Store in the fridge until ready to serve. It's good for up to 5 days.

Cherry Tomato, Broad Bean and Avocado Salsa

SERVES / 4

TIME TAKEN / 15 minutes

//

50g (1¾oz) fresh broad beans,
blanched, shelled and skins
discarded
100g (3½oz) cherry tomatoes, halved
1 small avocado, peeled, stoned
and diced
½ lemon zest and juice
4 tbsp olive oil, plus extra to drizzle
2 spring onions, finely sliced
½ bunch of fresh chopped coriander
sea salt and black pepper

Bring a pan of salted water to the boil. Blanch the broad beans by cooking them for 1 minute then refreshing them under cold running water. Once they are cool, peel the beans and discard the skins.

Put the peeled beans into a small mixing bowl with all the remaining salsa ingredients. Season with salt and pepper and gently mix.

Roast Corn Salsa

SERVES / 4

TIME TAKEN / 30 minutes

//

Corn salsa is the perfect
accompaniment to our corn fritters
(see page 86) and huevos rancheros
(see page 28). It's great with
scrambled eggs and cornbread too.

2 corn on the cob, husks removed
3 tbsp olive oil
½ red onion, finely diced
1 red pepper, finely diced
2 spring onions, finely sliced
½ red chilli, deseeded and
finely diced
30g (1¼oz) coriander, chopped
sea salt and black pepper

Preheat the oven to 170°C fan/190°C/375°F/gas 5.

Bring a large pan of water to the boil. Add the corn and cook for 4 minutes, then drain the cobs in a colander. Place the corn on a roasting tray, drizzle with 1 tablespoon of the olive oil and season. Roast for 8 minutes until starting to turn golden, then remove from the oven and allow to cool.

Once cool, remove the corn from the cob using a small serrated knife. Put it in a mixing bowl and add the red onion, pepper, spring onions, chilli, coriander and the remaining olive oil. Season to taste and mix well.

Salted Caramel

///

The method we use to make salted caramel does not require a sugar thermometer, but does require a careful eye to make sure it doesn't burn, which it can do in seconds.

MAKES / 500ml
TIME TAKEN / 25 minutes

200g (7oz) caster sugar
100ml (3½fl oz) golden syrup
300ml (10½fl oz) double cream
50g (1¾oz) unsalted butter, diced
½ tsp sea salt

Before you start, make sure you have all your ingredients ready to hand.

Heat the sugar and golden syrup in a medium-sized heavy-based pan over a medium heat. Keep stirring with a wooden spoon until the sugar dissolves and a dark amber liquid is formed. Keep a constant eye whilst doing this as the mixture can burn easily. The resulting liquid will be slightly darker than the golden syrup.

Slowly add the double cream to the caramelised sugar and syrup. Be careful so as to avoid splashing; as you're adding cold cream to a hot mixture, the mixture will bubble intensly. Cook for around 5 minutes until smooth and incorporated.

Add the butter and salt and whisk them into the mixture. Cook for a further 5 minutes until slightly thickened and a golden caramel.

Remove from the heat and pass the sauce through a metal strainer to remove any sugar crystals that might have formed.

Pour the caramel into a heatproof container and allow to cool completely before storing in the fridge. The refrigerated sauce will keep for up to 1 month.

Apple Compote

MAKES / a 500-g (1lb 2oz) jar

TIME TAKEN / 35 minutes

Apple compote is best served with lemon polenta cake (see page 118), but it's also delicious on porridge or granola and yoghurt. You don't want it to be completely smooth – its really nice to have soft pieces of apple mixed with the creamy purée that the broken-down the fruit will give.

3 Bramley cooking apples, peeled, cored and cut into 5cm (2in) dice
2 Granny Smith apples, peeled, cored and diced into 5cm (2in) dice
4 tbsp caster sugar
1 tsp vanilla extract

Put all the ingredients into a non-stick pan and add 6 tablespoons water. Mix over a low heat until the sugar starts to dissolve, then raise the heat to medium and cook for 10–12 minutes. Whilst cooking, the apples will start to break down, which will create a rich chunky compote. Make sure you keep stirring so that the mixture doesn't catch on the bottom of the pan, and don't let the apples colour.

Once ready, set aside to cool, then store in fridge until needed. It will keep, chilled, for up to a week.

Berry Compote

MAKES / 250g (9oz)

TIME TAKEN / 25 minutes

This berry compote is great with pancakes, French toast, porridge, granola or even just with a bowl of yoghurt or ice cream too. The list is endless.

250g (9oz) frozen mixed berries (use directly from the freezer, do not defrost)
½ tsp vanilla extract
25g (1oz) caster sugar
1 tsp lemon juice

Put all the ingredients in a small pan set over a low heat and bring to a simmer. Cook the berries for 15–20 minutes, stirring occasionally to ensure the mixture's not sticking to the pan. The compote will have a wonderful shine and be syrupy at this point.

Remove from the heat and allow to cool for 1 hour in the pan before transferring the compote to a plastic container or a jam jar to store. Refrigerate and serve when required. This will keep for 5 days in the fridge.

Kimchi

MAKES / 3–4 x 225g (8oz) jars

TIME TAKEN / 1 hour, plus draining

//

25g (1oz) Korean chilli powder
  (gochu garu)
1 thumb fresh ginger, peeled
10 garlic cloves
2 tbsp soy sauce
2 tbsp fish sauce
½ Chinese cabbage, finely sliced
½ cucumber peeled, halved deseeded
  and thinly sliced into semicircles
1 tbsp sea salt
1 tbsp sugar
1 bunch spring onions, sliced
2 apples peeled, cored, and julienned
1 carrot, peeled and grated
bunch of coriander with roots,
  finely chopped

First, make the paste. Using a stick blender or food processor, purée the chilli, ginger, garlic, soy sauce and fish sauce together until you have a smooth, thick paste.

Place the cabbage and cucumber in a colander, sprinkle with the salt and sugar and mix to make sure everything is well combined. Leave to drain for 2 hours.

In a bowl, mix the paste with the wilted cabbage and cucumber. Add the spring onions, apples, carrot and coriander and mix until combined.

Pour the kimchi into sterilised jars (see page 128) and refrigerate. It can be used straightaway, but it's much better if you leave it for at least 3 days. It will keep in the fridge for up to 3 months.

Roast Garlic Aioli

SERVES / 4

TIME TAKEN / 25 minutes

//

This aioli can be made without roasting the garlic, but this step really adds an amazing depth of flavour and makes the flavour of garlic a little more subtle.

4 garlic cloves
150ml (5fl oz) olive oil
2 egg yolks
1 tsp Dijon mustard
150ml (5fl oz) rapeseed oil
1 tbsp water
1 tsp lemon juice
½ tsp wholegrain mustard
sea salt

Preheat the oven 160°C fan/180°C/350°F/gas 4.

Put the garlic in a small roasting pan or ovenproof frying pan with 2 tablespoons of the olive oil. Roast for 10–15 minutes until softened, then remove from the oven and allow to cool.

Put the garlic, egg yolks and Dijon mustard into a food processor and blitz to a paste. With the processor still running, slowly drizzle in the remaining olive oil. It's important to be patient and add the oil slowly or the aioli may split and you'll need to start again. Once the olive oil is added, add the rapeseed oil, again, pouring it in slowly. You should now have a thick mayonnaise. Add the water and lemon juice while still blending. Season with salt and add the wholegrain mustard. Transfer to a small airtight container and refrigerate for up to 3 days.

Clarified Butter

MAKES / 350–400g (12–14oz)

TIME TAKEN / 45 minutes

Clarified butter is the liquid left after the milk proteins are removed from butter. What is left is almost 100% pure butter, which can be cooked at a higher temperature. As the butter is cooking, the milk solids will collect at the bottom of the pot and start browning. This forms a sediment which needs to be discarded.

500g (1lb 2oz) unsalted butter

//

Melt the butter in a pan over a low heat. Increase the heat to medium and heat until the butter reaches a gentle boil and starts to bubble. As it boils, a foam will form on the surface. Using a ladle, skim this foam off the surface as it forms, and discard. Keep doing this until no more foam appears.

The clarified butter is ready when the bubbling calms down; this means the water has evaporated. Remove from the heat and allow to cool slightly.

Pass the liquid through a cheesecloth to remove the sediment of milk solids that will have formed at the bottom of the pan during cooking. Pour the strained clarified butter into a sealable container. This will keep in the fridge for up to 6 months.

Rosemary Butter

MAKES / 60g

TIME TAKEN / 15 minutes

60g (2oz) unsalted butter
needles from 2 sprigs rosemary, finely chopped
½ red chilli, deseeded and finely chopped
2 garlic cloves, finely chopped

//

Melt the butter in a small pan and continue cooking until it has browned slightly, but not burnt: you will notice tiny specks of brown on the base of the pan when it is ready. This stage is very important; the butter should resemble a golden amber colour and have a nutty aroma. Once it's browned, set it aside to cool a little.

Add the chopped rosemary, chilli and garlic. Place the chilli butter back on the stove and cook for further 3 minutes to release the flavour of the rosemary, chilli and garlic. Pour the butter into a sealable container and store in the fridge for up to 2 months.

Use the butter in the Mushrooms and Spinach on Sourdough Toast (see page 42). It is also delicious poured over roasted squash or grilled tenderstem broccoli.

Honeycomb Butter

//

It's very important to use a large deep pot when making honeycomb as once the bicarbonate of soda is added it will expand and foam very quickly. The last thing you want is for it to overflow from the pot as its extremely hot and is a real pain to clean as it sets instantly once its hits a cooler service. Make sure the tray you pour it into is deep as it will continue to bubble and grow. It's best to have everything set and ready and take care when making honeycomb.

MAKES/ 1 log (around 10–15 portions)
TIME TAKEN / 25 minutes, plus 1½ hours cooling

175g (6oz) caster sugar
175g (6oz) golden syrup
1 tsp bicarbonate of soda
750g (1lb 10oz) unsalted butter, softened

Line a small deep oven tray or a loaf tin with parchment so it's completely covered.

Combine the sugar and golden syrup in a large, deep heavy-based pan. Place the pan over a low heat and cook for 5 minutes, or until the sugar has dissolved, stirring occasionally. Brush down the side of the pan with a pastry brush dipped in water to remove any sugar crystals.

Once the sugar has dissolved, increase the heat to high and bring to the boil. Cook without stirring for 5–8 minutes, or until the syrup reaches crack stage on a sugar thermometer (154°C / 309°F). Remove the pan from the heat, add the bicarbonate of soda and quickly stir using a wooden spoon until the bicarb is fully incorporated. The mixture will bubble and foam and you'll need to be fast, but also careful as the mixture is very hot.

Pour the honeycomb into the prepared tray and put in a cool dry place so that it can set and get crispy. This will take between 1–1½ hours.

Now it's the fun part! Remove the honeycomb from the tray, put in a large bowl and remove the parchment. Using one end of a rolling pin, smash the honeycomb into bitesize pieces. It's important it's not too chunky or it will be difficult to roll the butter later.

Add the butter to the honeycomb and mix together so that everything is well combined and you can see bitesize pieces of honeycomb running through the butter.

Cut a 35cm (14in) square piece of parchment and lay on a work surface. Spoon the honeycomb butter across the bottom edge of the parchment to form a long sausage – make sure you spread it out evenly as it will help make sure the butter roll is an even width. Roll the butter up in the parchment to form a log and twist the excess paper at each end to seal, so it looks like a cracker.

Refrigerate and cut a slice when needed. This will last in the fridge for at least 2 months.

Hollandaise

//

Making home-made hollandaise is very satisfying!
Once you achieve a creamy silky sauce you will be stoked!

MAKES / 4

TIME TAKEN / 50 minutes

2 large egg yolks
125g (4½oz) Clarified Butter
 (see page 151), melted
1 tsp lemon juice
a pinch of sea salt

FOR CLASSIC HOLLANDAISE

½ tsp rapeseed oil
½ banana shallot, sliced
½ garlic clove, chopped
1 bay leaf
1 sprig thyme
1 small sprig rosemary
4 black peppercorns
125ml (4fl oz) white wine vinegar
60ml (2fl oz) white wine

FOR YUZU HOLLANDAISE

2 tbsp yuzu juice

For classic hollandaise, heat a small pan over a medium heat. Add the rapeseed oil and fry the shallot for 1–2 minutes until softened.

Add the garlic, bay leaf, thyme and rosemary and cook for a further 1–2 minutes. Add the peppercorns, along with the vinegar and white wine and simmer for 10–15 minutes. Remove the reduction from the heat and allow to cool, then strain, discarding the solids. (If not using straight away, refrigerate until needed. This will keep for up to 3 months in the fridge.)

For both the hollandaises. Have a small pan of just simmering water at the ready.

Place the egg yolks and 1 tablespoon of the reduction into a deep glass or metal bowl that will fit over the pan (if you're making yuzu hollandaise, add the yuzu in the place of the reduction). Whisk for a few minutes, then put the bowl over the pan of simmering water making sure the water is not touching the bottom of the bowl. Whisk continuously until pale and thick, around 3–4 minutes.

Remove the pan from the heat and very slowly whisk in the melted butter, a little at a time, until it is all incorporated. If added too quickly the sauce may split, so patience is key. Once it is all added, you will have a silky, slightly thick hollandaise. Add the lemon juice and a pinch of salt. Keep in a warm place until needed.

Drinks
the
Sunday
Way

Carrot, Orange, Ginger and Passion Fruit Juice

//

MAKES / 2
TIME TAKEN / 10 minutes

6 large carrots, tops removed
7cm (2¾in) piece fresh ginger, peeled
4 juicy oranges, peeled and quartered
2 passion fruit

TIP

If you don't have a juicer, you could use a food processor. Blend all ingredients on a high speed, then strain into the jug through a fine sieve lined with a muslin cloth to remove the pulp.

Have a jug at the ready to catch the juice coming out of the juicer.

Add the carrots to the juicer, one at a time until they are all juiced, then put the ginger and the orange quarters through the juicer.

Once all ingredients are juiced, stir the juice in the jug well before pouring into 2 serving glasses. Cut the passion fruit in half and squeeze 1 into each glass, discarding the husks.

This drink is best served immediately, but can be kept for up to 24 hours in the fridge.

Morning Green Juice

//

SERVES / 2
TIME TAKEN / 10 minutes

4 Granny Smith apples, quartered and
  core removed
4 sticks celery
1 cucumber, peeled
2.5cm (1in) piece fresh ginger, peeled
1 large handful of baby spinach
30g (1¼oz) kale, stems removed
10 mint leaves

The juice will separate the longer it sits but don't worry – a quick stir will reincorporate the ingredients and it will still be just as yummy. If you don't have a juicer, you could use a food processor (see above).

Have a jug at the ready to catch the juice coming out of the juicer.

Place the apples into the juicer one at a time, followed by the celery sticks, cucumber, ginger, spinach, kale and mint.

Once all ingredients are juiced, stir the juice in the jug well before pouring into 2 serving glasses with ice.

This drink is best served immediately, but can be kept for up to 24 hours in the fridge.

Berry, Grape and Bee Pollen Smoothie

SERVES / 2

TIME TAKEN / 5 minutes

350g (12oz) frozen summer mixed berries
1 banana, peeled
juice of 4 oranges
10 seedless red grapes, plus optional
extra to serve
1 tbsp acai berry powder
2 tsp bee pollen
2 tsp cacao nibs

Put the berries, banana, orange juice, grapes and acai berry powder in a food processor and blend for 2–3 minutes until you have a thick consistency. This drink doesn't need to be super smooth – it's great to have some texture.

Pour the smoothie into 2 serving glasses and garnish with a generous sprinkle of cacao nibs and bee pollen. A few halved grapes on top add an extra bite to the smoothie, if you like.

Bloody Mary

SERVES / 2

TIME TAKEN / 15 minutes

50ml (2fl oz) vodka (optional)
500ml (17fl oz) organic tomato juice
4 tsp lemon juice
2 small celery sticks, washed and ends
trimmed, to garnish
a pinch of dried chilli flakes, to garnish
lemon slices, to garnish

FOR THE BLOODY MARY MIX

125ml (4fl oz) Worcestershire sauce
1 tsp wholegrain mustard
1 tsp finely grated fresh horseradish or
horseradish cream
a pinch celery salt
a pinch of smoked paprika
1 tsp Tabasco sauce
sea salt and black pepper

To make the Bloody Mary mix, put the Worcestershire sauce, mustard, horseradish, celery salt, paprika, Tabasco, and a pinch each of salt and pepper into a mixing bowl. Whisk until all the ingredients are fully incorporated.

Half fill 2 large glasses with ice, add 30ml (1fl oz) of the Bloody Mary mix and half the vodka (if using) to each glass and stir. Add half the tomato juice and lemon juice to each glass and stir well, making sure to fully mix the tomato juice into the Bloody Mary mix.

Garnish with a celery stick, lemon slices and a sprinkle of pepper and chilli flakes.

Any leftover Bloody Mary mix can be kept in the fridge for up to 2 weeks.

Sunday Lemonade

MAKES / 2.5 litres (88fl oz)
TIME TAKEN / 25 minutes,
plus cooling time

170g (6oz) caster sugar
170g (6oz) demerara sugar
1.8 litres (63fl oz) filtered water
380ml (13fl oz) freshly squeezed lemon juice,
  seeds removed but keep some pulp
fresh mint and lime wedges, to serve

//

Add both the sugars and 250ml (9fl oz) of the filtered
water to a small pan. Bring to the boil and stir until the
sugar has dissolved. Remove from the heat and allow to
cool. Once cooled, refrigerate until cold.

Put the chilled syrup, lemon juice and the remaining
water into a 3-litre (5-pint) jar, close the lid and shake.

Transfer into 1-litre (35fl oz) soda bottles and
refrigerate. Serve over ice with fresh mint and a slice
of lime. The lemonade should be stored in the fridge
for up to 5 days.

Watermelon and Lime Cooler

SERVES / 4
TIME TAKEN / 10 minutes

1.5kg (3lb 6oz) chilled seedless watermelon,
  skin removed and diced
juice of 4 limes, plus 4 wedges to serve
4 tbsp honey or agave syrup, plus extra
  to taste if needed
8 sprigs of mint, to serve

//

Put all the ingredients in a food processor and
blend for 2–3 minutes until all the watermelon is
broken down.

Strain through a fine strainer into a jug and stir again.
Taste the drink for sweetness – you can add a touch
more honey if it's too sour, but be careful not to over-
sweeten as this drink should be sharp and fresh.

Refrigerate for 1 hour, then serve in glasses over ice.
Serve each glass with a lime wedge and 2 fresh sprigs
of mint.

Lacto-fermented Raspberry Soda

//

This refreshing and fruity summer soda is a great way to use up the whey produced when making labneh. It cleverly uses fermentation to give the drink a natural fizz which both children and adults will love.

MAKES / 2 litres (70fl oz)
TIME TAKEN / 40 minutes, plus fermenting time

500g (1lb 2oz) organic raspberries (frozen are fine)
200g (7oz) cane sugar
2 litres (70fl oz) filtered water
125ml (4fl oz) whey (liquid drained from the Labneh, see page 142)

In a pan, simmer the raspberries, sugar and water over a low heat for 25–30 minutes. Remove from the heat and allow to cool completely.

Once the mixture has cooled, pass it through a fine strainer lined with a muslin cloth to remove all the pulp. Discard the pulp and you should be left with a deep red juice.

Pour the raspberry juice into a 3-litre (5-pint) jar with a screw top lid. Add the whey, put the lid on tightly and give it a good shake.

To start the fermentation process, store the jar of soda in a cool, dry place for 2 days. After this time, you will see the whey starting to take effect in the soda. Open the jar, there may be some white froth on the top of the

soda which can be skimmed and discarded. Stir with a large wooden spoon.

Transfer the soda into 2 x 1-litre bottles with lids. Store for a further 3 days in a cool dry place, opening the lids of the soda bottles once a day to let out the gas that the fermentation has created. This stage is called 'burping' and is very important as the soda needs to release the gasses so that the bottles don't explode.

After the 3 days the soda is ready and can be stored in the fridge. Once in the fridge the fermentation will slow down. Serve over ice and enjoy. The soda should be stored in the fridge for up to 2 weeks.

Index

Thanks

//

ALAN

I would like to take this opportunity to thank my business partner Terence Williamson – when we talk about food, ideas just naturally flow and that is very rare to find; many of *Sunday*'s creations have come from our short chats about food and flavours whilst doing service at the cafe. I'm also grateful to a dear friend, Bonny Sentrosi. You helped us so much when we started bro, it's not forgotten.

I need to give a huge thank you to my partner Beth Macinnes for always supporting and believing in me, your confidence gave me the chance to believe in myself. My awesome children Joshua, Niah and Zawi. You three are the reason I work so hard: you have also been a massive part of Sunday over the years and a huge motivator for me when it comes to cooking good food.

Also thanks to my Mum who has always been a great example for me to follow and showed me that through hard work you can achieve a lot. Auntie Munchie thank you for always involving me in cooking. As a kid your house was the hub for feeding our family and you played a massive part in me becoming a chef. My brother Neill, sisters Lauren and Shannon. all family and friends, I appreciate you lot to the fullest!

Big thanks to Jessica Axe from Quarto group for giving us the opportunity to create this book! Also thanks to Gemma Anderson.

And of course all the customers at *Sunday* who have been coming over the years for brunch, without you guys none of this would be possible so I am truly grateful. Peace and love.

TERENCE

My deepest thanks to the following people…
Firstly to my business partner Alan Turner, our hard working staff past and present.

In addition I owe an enormous amount of gratitude to Nazish Minhas for helping me put some of these recipes into writing, Patricia Niven for her great photography, Leaping lizards for our colourful attire and also to everyone at our publishers for giving us the chance to write this book.

ADDITIONAL THANKS

First thanks to some solid staff members we have had over the years who we are forever indebted too, your contribution to *Sunday* has been immense so we salute you all. Megan Haynes, Martha Gallagher, Hayley Harvey, Mai Izumitani, Fiona Moore, Nacer Benamer, Mohammed Nouno, Gierdre Seibokaite, Orlei Pereira, Alex Durlik, Barbara Gornicka, Pedro, Mahadienne and Emer Connolly.

To our suppliers Godreys Co. (meat), Newington Green Fruit and Vegetables, Greens Produce, Mash Purveyors (veg), M. W. Capture (fish), Kypros (Halloumi), Northiam Dairy, Barradale Eggs, Penny and Aika (Leaping Lizards) and lastly a special thanks to Caravan Coffee Roasters who have been suppling *Sunday* with outstanding coffee from the very beginning. It's been a real pleasure working with you guys.

THE PUBLISHER WOULD LIKE TO THANK

Leaping Lizards for supplying the colourful textiles used in the photography. *leaping-lizards.co.uk*

Maizu Studios by Mai Izumitani for the loan of their beautiful ceramics. *maizustudios.com*

First published in 2020 by Frances Lincoln Publishing,
an imprint of The Quarto Group.
The Old Brewery, 6 Blundell Street
London, N7 9BH,
United Kingdom
T (0)20 7700 6700
www.QuartoKnows.com

A catalogue record for this book is available from the
British Library.

ISBN 978 0 7112 4859 5
Ebook ISBN 978 0 7112 4860 1

10 9 8 7 6 5 4 3 2

P.11, 88: photo on the wall (c) Mariano Vivanco

COMMISSIONING EDITOR / Cerys Hughes
EDITOR / Charlotte Frost
DESIGNER / Isabel Eeles
PHOTOGRAPHER / Patricia Niven
PHOTOGRAPHER'S ASSISTANT / Sam Reeves
PRODUCTION CONTROLLER / Robin Boothroyd
PROPS AND FOOD STYLIST / Pip Spence
PUBLISHER / Jessica Axe

Printed in Slovenia